Prophet, Priest, & King

R. ALBERT MOHLER JR.

Prophet, Priest, & King

The Three Offices of Christ

B&H PUBLISHING
BRENTWOOD, TENNESSEE

Printed in China

979-8-3845-0442-9

Published by B&H Publishing Group
Brentwood, Tennessee

Dewey Decimal Classification: 232
Subject Heading: JESUS CHRIST—ROYAL OFFICE /
JESUS CHRIST—PRIESTHOOD /
JESUS CHRIST— PROPHETIC OFFICE

Cover design by Jennifer Allison, 513 TN LLC.
Title fonts by Zakharchenko Anna and DaryaKoM, Shutterstock. Author photo by Trevor Wheeker, by permission of the Southern Baptist Theological Seminary.

1 2 3 4 5 6 • 28 27 26 25

To my faculty colleagues at Boyce College and
The Southern Baptist Theological Seminary.
Thank you for more than thirty years of work together,
teaching together, learning together, being faithful together,
loving God's Word and the gospel of Jesus Christ together,
serving the church together, and shaping a generation of
wonderful students together, to the glory of God.

R. Albert Mohler Jr.

Acknowledgments

I deeply appreciate the many people who have shaped my understanding and appreciation of the Three Offices of Christ. So many sermons, books, lectures, and conversations live in my thoughts and have shaped my own understanding. To all I am thankful. In my office, several people play key roles in my work and productivity. These would include Caleb Shaw, Chief of Staff, Carlo Cicero, Director of Strategic Research, Graham Faulkner, Director of Communications, and Nick Mottola, Digital Content Coordinator. Carlo has been especially helpful in this project, and I am thankful. I am also very thankful to Anna Thomas and Allison Moldenhauer, who have added so much to our team.

A group of outstanding interns worked in my office during this time and I deeply appreciate their energy, kindness, interest, and great promise for Christian ministry and leadership. They include Ben Pinkston, Alex Richey, William Wolfe, Jacob Page, Christopher Parr, Austin Puckett, J. P. Shafer, Caleb Green, and Marc Cogan.

My sweet family has been both helpful and encouraging. As always, I am eager to thank my dear wife Mary, my constant and brilliant and faithful partner in all things. Her contributions to my life and work are beyond description, but not beyond my gratitude.

Contents

Christ as King

Introduction

For Christians throughout all ages, having a personal knowledge of Christ is essential for faithful Christian living. This is because faithfulness in and of itself requires that we have real knowledge of Christ. In other words, one must know who Christ is and what Christ has done for us, in order to ground our faith in Christ. Add to that now, that faithful Christian living flows from faithful believing and thinking driven by a love for Christ. We know the way we live inevitably emerges out of our deepest *thoughts* and *beliefs* (Prov. 4:23; Matt. 12:34–35), and thus the Christian must not only have knowledge of Christ but must also engage the disciplines of thinking about and believing the truths about Christ in order to be faithful.

As a theologian and professor, I believe teaching such spiritual disciplines as thinking, believing, and living calls for an explicit affirmation and exposition of the three offices of Christ. Jesus decisively fulfilled the offices of prophet, priest, and king in his earthly life. Even in our day, now two millennia from the time of Christ's earthly ministry, the implication of his work continues to reverberate.

Today, we experience the tensions of the post-Christian, secular environment framing the world around us. Yet, when our faith remains grounded in Christ and thoroughly informed by his prophetic, priestly, and kingly offices, we need not be shaken by the subversions of the modern world. Because of Christ's work, we need not lose our firm footing or our meditation. When we consider these truths, our confidence and conviction grow, fueled by what Christ accomplished in his fulfillment of these offices. The tumult of the world drives us to a further understanding of Christ's work, and an understanding of Christ's work helps us withstand amid the storms of an increasingly secular age—an age that threatens to subvert the church's obedience to Christ.

We might ask ourselves, What consequential realities now exist for the Christian since Christ is our prophet, priest, and king? Not only that, but how ought we to apply these truths in order to live more faithfully to God in our contemporary moment? The answer to these questions requires our careful attention.

In preparing to consider Christ's offices, we do well to recall that an important history undergirds why we even speak of them in the first place. As we look back to the earliest centuries of Christianity, we find that the early church made reference to these three offices. Eusebius, after establishing the historicity of the three anointed Old Testament offices,[1] wrote of Jesus:

> But the great and convincing evidence of that incorporeal and divine power in him is the fact that he alone, of all that have ever existed to the present day, even now is known by the title of

> Christ among all men over the world; and with this title he is acknowledged and professed by all and celebrated both among barbarians and Greeks. Even to this day, he is honored by his followers throughout the world as a King; he is admired as more than a prophet and glorified as the only true High Priest of God. In addition to all these, as the preexisting Word of God, coming into existence before all ages, and who has received the honors of worship, he is also adored as God.[2]

Our understanding of Christ as mediating these three offices is deeply rooted in the Scriptures but became particularly important during the Protestant Reformation. Specifically, John Calvin, the great reformer of Geneva, made some of the most meaningful advancements to our understanding of Christ's three offices in his magisterial work *The Institutes of the Christian Religion* (Book II, chapter 15). In this sixteenth century theological treatise, he sought to offer the best biblical exposition of Christ's work, and in doing so, Calvin clearly defined Christ's three offices. He also showed the continuity of these offices between the Old and New Testaments, and he demonstrated how Christ ultimately and infinitely fulfilled each of these offices through his earthly ministry and his eternal kingdom.

Yet, in all of Calvin's explication, he did not go so far as to suggest that one may segregate Christ's offices into discrete and separate ministries. One cannot compartmentalize Christ's offices. An analogy with the person and work of Christ proves helpful here. When we consider the person and the work of Jesus

Christ, we rightly make a distinction in our theological thinking between the two, and at the same time, we realize that no ultimate or absolute division between the two exists. Said another way, when we speak of Christ's person, we necessarily speak of his work, and to speak of his work requires the affirmation of his person as revealed in Scripture—something the church has confessed throughout the ages. Similarly, when we speak of Christ's three offices, we cannot speak of them as if each or any exists entirely independent of the others. Rather, we rightly recognize something important in what Calvin identified as the threefold office of Christ. He said, "Therefore, in order that faith may find a firm basis for salvation in Christ, and thus rest in him, this principle must be laid down: the office enjoined upon Christ by the Father consists of three parts. For he was given to be a prophet, king, and priest."[3] So, interconnected within Christ's ministry, Calvin conceived of Christ fulfilling his prophetic, priestly, and kingdom work through a single office having three aspects. Though distinguished, they remain inseparable, even as Christ is indivisible.

Another important observation concerning Christ's offices that originated during the Reformation is that affirming the three offices of Christ does not merely provide a helpful—or even necessary—way of understanding and explaining the work of Christ. The affirmation moves beyond offering information. Rather, asserting that Christ holds the offices of Prophet, Priest, and King also makes a theological argument.

Martin Luther, another great Protestant reformer, plainly articulated this when he spoke of what makes someone a true a theologian. In his commentaries he declared, "Living, or rather dying and being damned makes a theologian, not understanding, reading, or speculating."[4] Luther meant that a Christian moves into the faithfulness of being a theologian not by ivory tower musings or hypotheticals about God but through a crucible. In that crucible we confront the reality of our own sin and recognize what is at stake in such matters—our absolute dependence on Christ for salvation. Luther said the theologian lives by assertions.[5] He does not content himself by making suggestions or merely offering explanations on matters of faith. Instead, he lives by making assertions about both what is true and what must therefore follow as a result of that truth. When we speak of Christ as prophet, Christ as priest, and Christ as king, we make the assertion that Christ is indeed the Prophet, that Christ is in every way our Great High Priest, and that Christ is King of kings and Lord of lords. The implications of such truths cannot carry greater significance. There we see the glory of Jesus Christ our Lord displayed in triple magnificence.

Looking at the three offices collectively makes more of an argument than one might think. For instance, many associated with liberal Protestantism wanted to speak only of Christ as prophet. In the reductionism of Protestant liberalism, its practitioners denied Christ as priest or even the need for Christ as priest. They dismissed substitutionary atonement—redemption on a cross or "bloody cross religion," as some of the liberals called it. They also turned Christ as king into something merely political. What they wanted to hold onto reduced Christ to a moral teacher because they could not bear the argument implicit in Christ's existing as priest and as eternal king.

Another argument surfaces among some of those who do believe in an earthly priesthood. Think of the priestly churches and denominations in the world, with the Roman Catholic church as prime example. The centrality of a human priesthood undermines the priestly role of Christ—a solitary role. Christ as priest made atonement for sin once for all. He sits at the right hand of God the Father Almighty and is forever interceding for us, his saints. Make no mistake about it. Christ's fulfilling his office of priest makes an argument, and it is an argument basic and necessary to the faithful Christian faith.

On the other hand, evangelical Christianity sometimes neglects Christ as prophet and as king. Some evangelicals emphasize Christ as priest while diminishing the other offices. It is common to speak of the gospel, the cross of Christ, the empty tomb, and Christ's resulting priestly ministry without really understanding what it means to speak of Christ as our Great High Priest. And in this moment, still fewer evangelicals seem to grasp Christ as prophet and Christ as king. It is high time for a theological recovery.

One of the tensions we see in contemporary evangelicalism involves an unease over what it means for us to proclaim that Jesus Christ is Lord, that Jesus Christ reigns supremely as King over all, and that we exist—even now—as citizens of his heavenly kingdom. This reality requires us to recognize our ultimate identity as citizens of the kingdom of God and that our most basic allegiance is to Christ as King. In a moment of all kinds of questions among evangelicals—including tensions and controversies about political responsibility—we can offer our fellow Christian brothers and sisters one of the healthiest means of encouragement in Christ by looking them in the eye and proclaiming that a follower of the Lord Jesus Christ recognizes only one King and only one eternal kingdom. We fundamentally and unconditionally commit ourselves to Christ and to his rule. In light of his person and work, we need to consider Jesus, and we need to deepen and further develop our understanding of him as he fulfills his three offices of prophet, priest, and king.

The best way to approach each of Christ's three offices, or even the generalized structure of understanding the three-fold offices of Christ, is to move continually between the Old Testament and the New Testament and draw connections of promise and fulfillment between the two testaments. In other words, we embark on a biblical and theological examination of these offices. To speak of the three offices of Christ in the context of biblical theology means we refuse to unhitch the church from the Old Testament. Pursuing a biblical theology of Christ's three offices does exactly the opposite. We know this because such a course of study demonstrates how Christ defined his own ministry, person, and work from the totality of Scripture. Jesus is the perfect fulfillment of the Old Testament promise of the Messiah.

We do not hesitate to take this direction, for Jesus himself calls for it. He reminded his listeners that the Old Testament Scriptures bore witness of him (John 5:39). Then he went on to say that "if you believed Moses, you would believe me, because he wrote about me" (John 5:46). On yet another occasion, Jesus told the parable in Luke 16 of the rich man and Lazarus, in which the rich man crying out to Abraham, says, "'Father,' he said, 'then I beg you to send him to my father's house—because I have five brothers—to warn them, so that they won't also come to this place of torment'" (Luke 16:27–28). As Jesus tells the account, "Abraham said, 'They have Moses and the prophets; they should listen to them'" (Luke 16:29). And though the rich man said, "But if someone from the dead goes to them, they will repent" (Luke 16:30), Abraham responds conclusively, "If they don't listen to Moses and the prophets, they will not be persuaded if someone rises from the dead" (Luke 16:31). In Jesus's self-declaration, the Scriptures have long spoken of his significance and ministry, and they continue to demand our careful consideration.

Our task, then, in grasping Jesus's fulfillment of his prophetic, priestly, and kingly offices must span the full scope of God's Word. As we look at patterns of promise and fulfillment, type and reality, we will find ourselves unashamedly making an argument. We will also find ourselves drawn into a deeper worship of Christ. For through our meditation on his Word, we come to know him more fully, in his glory, power, dominion, and majesty.

CHRIST AS

PROPHET

While the Old Testament priest mediated before God on behalf of his people—as we will see in the next chapter—the prophet communicated the word of God to the people of God. An office inaugurated in the Old Testament, the prophet was called God's messenger not simply for mankind in general but for God's people, for *Israel.* Scripture foretells a messianic prophet who will declare the word of God to his people *and* save them from their sins. This is especially apparent in the Gospels, where Jesus both fulfills and transcends the biblical mandate of a prophet. He is the incarnate Word whom the prophets of old proclaimed.

Chapter 1

The Prophet Today

Of these three offices of prophet, priest, and king, the prophet is the one most commonly referenced in our contemporary moment. For many without a biblical worldview, the prophet offers a secular gospel of hope. The prophet declares an eschaton which contrasts with a disappointing, mediocre world. As one writer has observed, Steve Jobs is a quintessential example of a secular prophet in recent years, a man whose "most singular quality was his ability to articulate a perfectly secular form of hope." Through his technological innovation, the apple with a bite taken out of it—formerly a symbol of man's fall—became an icon of the fulfilled life.[6] Central to a prophet's mission is his philosophy, a vision of the good life. For technocrats like Jobs, the prophecy is of a transhumanist world which transcends physical limitations.

Other secular prophets claim to confront social justice and oppression with truth, facing any cost. One thinker envisions a prophet who critically examines—then courageously fights—injustice. He summarizes the prophetic voice in this way: "For each of you, there is something inside, a voice that won't let you hold your peace, something in the world that you want to be better. . . . Find that something more that lures us out of our earthbound clay feet existence and into truthful acts of courage."[7] For some, social justice activists prophesy the message of universal virtues when they resist systems of power and oppression. Sometimes, in the name of tolerance, these activists elevate priorities like diversity, equity, and inclusion in such a way as to declare virtues of the Christian faith anathema.

Many evangelicals also misunderstand prophecy when they unintentionally limit the prophet's work to prediction of future events. Perhaps the modern phenomenon which best illustrates this is the "prophecy conference," where people gather to hear a teacher explain how the events of today's front page align with prophecies in Daniel and Revelation. One such event describes itself as a "live prophetic event" where the teacher will describe what "the Lord is revealing to him at this time" regarding "the Word of prophecy, the last days, the return of Christ, and what the Holy Spirit is saying."[8] An emphasis on prophecy in this way is unhelpful and misleading when it is disconnected from a commitment to the sole authority of Scripture.

A biblical understanding of the prophet's role certainly includes the foretelling of future events, for Scripture is replete with predicative prophecies. These give rise to the general structure of *promise and fulfillment* recognized throughout the Bible. In fact, the entirety of the Old Testament fits within the pattern of promise just as the whole of the New Testament fits within the pattern of fulfilment. With that said, however, the most important responsibility of the Old Testament prophet did not really entail *foretelling* so much as it entailed *forthtelling*. He was to profess, proclaim, and put forth God's message. God identified the prophet as his messenger, a teacher of truth and righteousness, and he made central to the prophetic responsibility not only declaring the truth but also calling all to repentance.

The words of Isaiah 40:5 poignantly exemplify the distinguishing voice of the biblical prophet: "And the glory of the LORD will appear, and all humanity together will see it, for the mouth of the LORD has spoken." Secular prophets attempt to speak their own truth to power, but the biblical prophets proclaimed divine revelation, *God's* message to *his* people. Secular prophets have no need of revelation, Scripture, or a Word from God. The prophets of today may have much to say, but the only guide they can offer is themselves. Yet for God's prophet, the Word of God from the mouth of God is the sure and sufficient message.

God has sent many prophets to his people over the course of biblical history. The apostle Paul goes so far as to identify those prophets, along with the apostles, as the foundation upon which the church is built. Nonetheless, as he continues, "Christ Jesus himself as the cornerstone. In him the whole building, being put together, grows into a holy temple in the Lord" (Eph. 2:20–21). The final and ultimate prophet is the very Word of whom the prophets of the Old Testament spoke and foretold. In contrast to false prophets, Jesus does not speak of a new humanist worldview, or power gained in magical victory over perceived oppressors. Christ declares the word of salvation and the coming kingdom of God. Throughout the Old and New Testaments, Scripture consistently presents Christ's unique office as the messianic prophet, a vision that truly transforms and strengthens Christians today.

Chapter 2

The Old Testament: The Messianic Prophet Foretold

A diligent search of the Old Testament reveals both messianic anticipations of a coming prophet and the corresponding expectations of the one who would fulfill this role. These findings underline the recognition that Christ's offices as prophet, priest, and king express his saving and ruling work as the Messiah. The Messiah holds not just one office; he holds all three of them.

Deuteronomy 18 introduces the anticipation and promise of a messianic prophet, though not all is immediately revealed in any one text.

> The Lord your God will raise up for you a prophet like me from among your own brothers. You must listen to him. This is what you

> requested from the Lord your God at Horeb on the day of the assembly when you said, "Let us not continue to hear the voice of the Lord our God or see this great fire any longer, so that we will not die!" Then the Lord said to me, "They have spoken well. I will raise up for them a prophet like you from among their brothers. I will put my words in his mouth, and he will tell them everything I command him. I will hold accountable whoever does not listen to my words that he speaks in my name. But the prophet who presumes to speak a message in my name that I have not commanded him to speak, or who speaks in the name of other gods—that prophet must die." (vv. 15–20)

Part of the *deuteronomos*, or the second giving of the Law, Moses here delivers a sermon designed to prepare the children of Israel to live in covenant faithfulness as they take the land and claim God's promise. This second, younger generation had not sinned in the wilderness in the way the first generation did. Thus, they will enter Canaan. Moses knew that he would not lead Israel into the land—for God gave this charge to Joshua—but he remained God's prophet, and so he continued to serve Israel for the length of his days. He still taught God's Word to God's people, and as he did so, he proclaimed that "the Lord your God will raise up for you a prophet like me from among your own brothers. You must listen to him" (Deut. 18:15). Moses explained that another will come after him. This individual will come from Israel, he will resemble Moses, he will fulfill the office of prophet, and all of God's people must hear him.

Some readers of the passage may be unaware that it necessarily predicts a messianic prophet who would not appear until the New Testament. They might assert that an entire succession of prophets came after Moses, and that specific succession amounted to the fulfillment of Moses's declaration. For example, the medieval Jewish commentator Nachmanides fails to speculate on the future identity of this prophet, only asserting that he will come out of the land of Israel and will be a true prophet of God (who has put his spirit only on Israel, not on other lands).[9] *Indeed*, a succession of prophets did come after Moses who spoke God's word to Israel. However, that succession by itself did not and cannot fulfill the prophetic fullness of Deuteronomy 18 in an ultimate sense. Consider the final verses of Deuteronomy. In Deuteronomy 34, Moses has died, and Joshua has taken on his responsibilities.

> No prophet has arisen again in Israel like Moses, whom the Lord knew face to face. He was unparalleled for all the signs and wonders the Lord sent him to do against the land of Egypt—to Pharaoh, to all his officials, and to all his land—and for all the mighty acts of power and terrifying deeds that Moses performed in the sight of all Israel. (vv. 10–12)

Among the succession of prophets that followed Moses, none had yet arisen with so intimate a relationship with God. None had yet come with a ministry so characterized by signs, wonders, and mighty deeds. None had yet performed such works in utter opposition to the forces of darkness and death and in the sight of God's people. Moses still exceeded these others. His prophetic ministry stood apart, and yet one like unto Moses would come, and a prophet far greater than Moses would appear.

Chapter 3

The New Testament: The Messianic Prophet Incarnate

The New Testament demonstrates that Christ was that ultimate prophet yet to come. One aspect of his office is his proclamation of a godly ethic. The philosopher pursues wisdom and "enables people to see the world in a certain way and to live accordingly."[10] This task is shared with the prophet, who communicates a vision of the good life which is directly given and revealed by God. One scholar has sought to demonstrate that both "the Old Testament prophets were philosophers," and "Jesus was the greatest philosopher."[11] Christ fulfills the office of prophet by communicating a righteous way of living in the world which first and foremost loves and obeys God in heart and mind.

The theme of living rightly is present throughout the prophetic literature of the Old Testament, with the first chapters of Isaiah describing the tragic results of abandoning obedience. Israel, the people of God, has rejected God. "Oh sinful nation, people weighed down with iniquity, brood of evildoers, depraved children! They have abandoned the LORD; they have despised the Holy One of Israel; they have turned their backs on him" (Isa. 1:4). God calls Isaiah as a prophet to rebuke Israel for their spiritual adultery and return to following God and his ways in their lives. He will be sent to a people of unclean lips, those who fail to hear God. The people do not repent, and their hearts remain dull. Nonetheless, the prophetic call to repentance will urge them to change their ways in accordance with God's revealed will (Isa. 6:8–10).

Jesus most clearly manifests his prophetic ministry in a similar fashion in the Sermon on the Mount. At the end of Jesus's discourse, the text notes, "When Jesus had finished saying these things, the crowds were astonished at his teaching, because he was teaching them like one who had authority, and not like their scribes" (Matt. 7:28–29). Jesus always spoke with an uncommon and singular authority. He did not speak in the manner of the scribes, who, like the secular prophets of today, proposed truth of their own authority (Matt. 7:29). While the scribes might have claimed to interpret Scripture, Jesus himself uttered Scripture. John 1 provides the reason for this distinction: "In the beginning was the Word, and the Word was with God, and the Word was God. He was with God in the beginning" (John 1:1–2). Jesus, the messianic prophet, communicated God's word like the prophets of old. However, John highlights the fact that this prophet is no *mere* prophet. Jesus is the incarnate Word whom the true prophets proclaimed. Our God teaches us how to read and understand the Bible.

One of the most popular homiletical texts of the 1970s was *As One without Authority*, written by preaching professor Fred Craddock and based on his Beecher Lectures at Yale University. Presenting a new mode of preaching for a secular age, his motives are made clear by his title. His was a new view of preaching and authority which diminished the traditional emphasis on the Word of God in Scripture, identifying new authorities and frames of reference:

> Rarely, if ever, in the history of the church have so many firm periods slumped into commas and so many triumphant exclamation marks curled into question marks. Those who speak with strong conviction on a topic are suspected of the heresy of premature finality. Permanent temples are to be abandoned as houses of idolatry; the true people of God are in tents again. It is the age of journalistic theology; even the Bible is out in paperback.[12]

A couple of pages later, he spoke of younger pastors and said,

> As a rule, younger ministers are keenly aware of the factors discussed above, and their preaching reflects it. Their predecessors ascended the pulpit to speak of the eternal certainties, truths etched forever in the granite of absolute reality, matters framed for proclamation, not for discussion. But where have all the absolutes gone?

> The old thunderbolts rust in the attic while the minister tries to lead his people through the morass of relativities and proximate possibilities, and the difficulties involved in finding and articulating a faith are not the congregation's alone; they are the minister's as well. How can he preach with a changing mind? How can he, facing new situations by the hour, speak the approximate word? He wants to speak and yet he needs more time for more certainty before speaking. His is often the misery of one who is always pregnant but never ready to give birth.[13]

Craddock makes these assertions because he identified no definitive word from the Lord. For him, the certainty of Jesus and generations of preachers in the past is gone. Craddock was undoubtedly eloquent, powerfully describing the necessary, new modern faith as "periods slumping into commas, and exclamation marks simply curling into question marks." However, there is no surety in a gospel of commas and question marks. This is merely the gospel of the scribes reincarnated for the present age. The true gospel is steadfast in its confidence in Christ's atonement for sin and the redemption of his church. There is no salvation in commas. Salvation is a sentence that ends in an exclamation point.

In the middle of the sermon, Jesus expands upon God's commands in the Old Testament Law, further expressing his prophetic office. He structures his statements in a familiar pattern, "You have heard that it was said . . . but I say to you" (Matt. 5:21–38 ESV). By saying this, Jesus in no way liberated

Christians from the Old Testament. He made it more excruciatingly demanding given his authority as the promised Prophet, Redeemer, and Second Person of the Trinity. Jesus highlighted the *interior* nature of sin—lust, adultery, anger, or otherwise—and taught that the Christian's holy posture must be a heart submitted to God's will. It is not enough to focus merely on external actions. Sin is inside as well.

Christ explains that a person who simply avoids committing adultery in the body still does not measure up to the standard of sexual purity. One ought not even lust after another person. Likewise, someone who simply refrains from murdering another individual still does not meet the standard of godly relations with one's neighbor. One ought not even to have anger in the heart toward a neighbor. Jesus teaches that human righteousness must emerge from a renewed heart, one characterized by love for God and neighbor. The righteousness that emerges from within—as an expression of that person's true nature—must exceed the outward and hypocritical righteousness of the scribes and Pharisees (Matt. 5:20). The prophetic lens of promise and fulfillment is echoed in Jesus's statements. God teaches his people the law of Christ through the inner workings of the Holy Spirit just as he promised he would (Isa. 54:13; Jer. 31:31–34). The Sermon on the Mount displays the law of Christ and highlights Jesus as God's true prophet teaching with authority.

Chapter 4

Christ's Miracles and His Prophetic Office

Christ's prophetic office extends beyond his teaching and his words, though Peter was right to identify Jesus's words as the unchanging source of truth and salvation: "Lord, to whom will we go? You have the words of eternal life" (John 6:68). In everything Jesus brought forth revelation. Whether through his teaching, miracles, even in his passion, Christ proclaimed the gospel.

Christ's miracles had prophetic significance to his disciples. This aspect of his prophetic ministry is evident in John 6, which recounts a series of events which reveal that Christ's actions serve to fulfill his messianic office. A survey of these accounts demonstrates the prophetic character of Jesus's incarnation and life. As the Chalcedonian Creed (AD 451) rightly affirms, Jesus is both truly God and truly man; his acts inherently represent God and declare God's message to the people.

Jesus's feeding of the five thousand at the beginning of John 6 demonstrates his prophetic care for God's people. After prompting his disciples to seat a large crowd, he took up five barley loaves and two fish from a boy among the multitude. Then he gave thanks, multiplied the bread and fish, and handed out a surplus so great that no one among the vast throng went hungry. The disciples even gathered up twelve baskets of leftovers after the meal (John 6:12–13), and this miraculous event did not go unnoticed.

As the Passover approached (John 6:4), the people of Israel would have observed the connections between God's provision for them through Moses and Jesus's even greater work. Just as Moses's intercession brought food in the wilderness (Exod. 16; Num. 11), so Jesus miraculously provided sustenance. His actions were indicative of his status as a messianic prophet. Moses interceded to God on behalf of the people, and God subsequently supplied the food. In Jesus's miracle, however, this crowd had eaten because Jesus supplied the meal himself. Amazed by Christ's miraculous provision, the people concluded that Jesus "is indeed the Prophet who is to come into the world!" and they sought to make him king (John 6:14–15 ESV). They saw him working the works of God and fulfilling the expectations of the messianic prophet, and they moved to crown him as their sovereign. As Jesus knew his full identity was not yet to be revealed, he quickly departed the scene, continuing to demonstrate his prophetic role day by day with his disciples.

Christ walking on water to his disciples on the Sea of Galilee (John 6:16–19) is reminiscent of Moses's splitting the Red Sea (Exod. 13–15). Jesus displayed an absolute and personal authority over creation. Moses defied the Egyptians and delivered his people because God had empowered him with sanction over the waters. Now the waters obey Jesus's authority, upholding his every step. The divine Creator—incarnate in human flesh—walks on his own creation. Even in his might, Christ exhibits prophetic care for the disciples, representing God in human flesh before them. Even his response to the disciples, "It is I. Don't be afraid." (John 6:20), recalls the great I AM of Exodus 3:14 and Moses's extraordinary encounter with him. "God replied to Moses, 'I AM WHO I AM.'" And he said, "This is what you are to say to the Israelites: I AM has sent me to you'" (Exod. 3:14).

Throughout the Gospel of John, a succession of "I am" statements demonstrate Christ's fulfillment of his prophetic office by revealing his identity and attributes. He is the bread of life, (John 6:35), the light of the world (John 8:12; 9:5), the door of the sheep (John 10:7), the good shepherd (John 10:11, 14), the resurrection and the life (John 11:25), the way, the truth, and the life (John 14:6), and the true vine (John 15:1), and each aspect serves to fill out his divine identity and his messianic purpose.

In John 6, Jesus declares, "I am the bread of life." As the crowd followed Jesus, he said to them, "Truly I tell you, you are looking for me, not because you saw the signs, but because you ate the loaves and were filled" (John 6:26). Jesus knows that this crowd now seeks him out because they want another meal, so he exhorts them not to "work for the food that perishes but for the food that lasts for eternal life, which the Son of Man will give you, because God the Father has set his seal of approval on him" (John 6:27). In other words, by coming to Jesus looking simply to fill their stomachs, they look for the wrong kind of bread. They were satisfied all too easily. The crowds recognized Jesus's prophetic fulfillment in feeding the five thousand, but they did not see that in this act he also prefigured his infinitely greater work of atonement to come.

From the beginning of John's Gospel, John has presented Jesus as a prophet like Moses but one with a greater and final fulfillment of the prophetic office. Moses brought forth God's instruction, but Jesus incarnates and brings forth God's grace and truth (John 1:17). Now, Jesus delivers God's message of grace and truth that he, himself, is the bread of life. When Jesus says this, he makes a clear claim to deity reflective of a passage like Exodus 3:13–14. As the Father fed his people in the wilderness, he now gives his Son such that all who partake of this heavenly manna experience the new and greater exodus. All who share in the Son find eternal life, but they must listen to his prophetic word. They must come and believe his gospel message.

From the beginning of this gospel, John intends that his readers make a decision regarding belief in Christ. John writes: "In the beginning was the Word" (John 1:1), and that the Word is the one who "became flesh and dwelt among us" (John 1:14). The one who was with God *was God*, and through whom all things were made (John 1:1–2). All such truths are crucial to understanding and receiving Jesus's message of good news. If Jesus is the bread of life, belief in him is required for eternal fellowship with God.

John 6:40 contains language similar to John 3:16, that verse so familiar to us. Those within earshot must now heed the will of the Father and listen to God's anointed prophet who himself feeds God's people. The prophet of God regularly speaks to a rebellious, grumbling people who have ignored God's message. Just as many complained against Moses, Elijah, Jeremiah, and others, when the messianic prophet issued his proclamation,

"The Jews started grumbling about him because he said, 'I am the bread that came down from heaven.' They were saying, 'Isn't this Jesus the son of Joseph, whose father and mother we know? How can he now say, 'I have come down from heaven'?" (John 6:41–42). The Bible classifies grumbling as one of the worst and most subversive of sins. The children of Israel in the older generation grumbled in the wilderness, and that led them to God's judgment and a state of perpetual wandering in the wilderness until they died. Because of this, Jesus's answer, "Stop grumbling among yourselves," demonstrates the seriousness of his statement (John 6:43). Rejecting Christ as the bread of life is a rejection of God himself. To reject Jesus and his ministry is to be like the wilderness generation once again.

Notice the repetition of Jesus's bread of life statements. Three times in this section he tells them he is the bread of life. In verse 35 we read, "'I am the bread of life,' Jesus told them. 'No one who comes to me will ever be hungry, and no one who believes in me will ever be thirsty again.'" In verse 41, in response to the Jews grumbling, he said, "'I am the bread that came down from heaven.'" Then, in verse 48, Jesus repeats in its simplest, most essential form, "I am the bread of life," Christ's repetition is nothing less than a call to repentance. This generation, like their fathers before them, fails to believe what is right in front of them. They are told once, twice, even three times, and still grumbling unbelief is in their heart.

Though this generation is like the wilderness generation, they are also unlike them. For while their fathers ate of a heavenly physical provision, that bread could not sustain them eternally. This is where Jesus turns in the third of his declarations. After saying, "I am the bread of life" (John 6:48), Jesus says,

"Your ancestors ate the manna in the wilderness, and they died. This is the bread that comes down from heaven so that anyone may eat of it and not die" (John 6:49–50). Jesus's listeners responded to physical food yet ignored the infinitely more significant spiritual food.

Human beings often take the lesser rather than the greater. Herein is one of the great themes of literature—even a picture of humanity. On our own, human beings tend to reject the greater and choose the lesser. We have very real appetites. We experience real hunger in our stomach. This conflict can be seen in the Old Testament between Jacob and Esau but also in our own lives. We are tempted to choose the temporary over the eternal. We are satisfied for a moment with bread even when we are presented with the bread of life.

Just a few verses earlier, Jesus articulates what R. C. Sproul rightly referenced as the "universal negative proposition" of the gospel.[14] These verses explain precisely why some do not reject Jesus and instead find salvation in him. First, in verse 37, there is the positive statement of the gospel: "Everyone the Father gives me will come to me, and the one who comes to me I will never cast out" (John 6:37). Then, Jesus issues the "universal negative proposition" in verse 44 asserting, "No one can come to me unless the Father who sent me draws him, and I will raise him up on the last day" (John 6:44). The two of these are essentially connected.

John 6 clarifies that the only proper response to the prophetic word is faith, resulting from the regeneration by the Spirit. So Jesus continues, "It is written in the Prophets: And they will all be taught by God" (John 6:45). In the context of his own ministry and in the midst of his own declaration of his saving identity as the bread of life, Jesus cites Isaiah's promise that "then all your children will be taught by the LORD, their prosperity will be great" (Isa. 54:13). By referencing that specific statement of the prophet and then saying that all people who hear and learn from the Father come to him, Jesus explains those who do and those who do not hear his prophetic word. He explains those who are and are not saved. The Father teaches, or makes alive, some and not others, and only a few verses later, Jesus adds that the Holy Spirit serves as the operating explanation:

> "The Spirit is the one who gives life. The flesh doesn't help at all. The words that I have spoken to you are spirit and are life. But there are some among you who don't believe." (For Jesus knew from the beginning those who did not believe and the one who would betray him.) He said, "This is why I told you that no one can come to me unless it is granted to him by the Father." (John 6:63–65)

The Spirit of God makes alive. Apart from him faith is inoperative. Flesh in this sense describes the principle of human sinfulness including even human self-righteousness, which in God's economy equates to filthy rags (Isa. 64:6). Yet the Spirit gives life. He works to make one live, meaning that he gives salvation. Scripture teaches clearly that no one can believe until that moment of illumination by the act of the Holy Spirit. Regeneration comes when that opening of the eyes leads to faith in Christ—we then feed on the Bread of Life.

The Westminster Shorter Catechism rightly asserts that "Christ executeth the office of a prophet, in revealing to us, by his word and Spirit, the will of God for our salvation."[15] Jesus declares that his words contain life, and herein we find the gospel message—the words of spirit and the words of life. This is why Jesus said that no one will come to him unless the Father grants it. The Father instructs the hearts of men to believe on the Son through the working of the Holy Spirit. God alone remains the initiator of belief, and so some hear his word while others do not. Some refuse Jesus's prophetic word and turn back (John 6:66). This is Jesus's prophetic ministry revealed: in the preaching the gospel of new life in him and in the massive revelatory disclosure of God's sovereignty in human salvation.

As John 6 draws to a close and many disciples no longer walk with him, Jesus asks the twelve, "You don't want to go away too, do you?" (John 6:67). Then Peter replies, "Lord, to whom will we go? You have the words of eternal life. We have come to believe and know that you are the Holy One of God" (John 6:68–69). The language of "words" is prophetically significant. Six times in Deuteronomy 18:15–22 the prophet is characterized as one who brings words. More specifically, God's prophet brings God's words. Here in John 6, Peter says, "You have the words of eternal life" (v. 68). When Jesus asked Peter and the disciples if they too will depart, the reader can imagine Peter's deduction. "How did we hear of salvation? We had to hear of salvation from you, Jesus. Prophets of old had foretold the promise, but you fulfill both the prophets and the prophecy. Not only that, but you now come even as the long-awaited and promised prophet, and so when you ask, 'Will you now also go away?,' we disciples must answer, we will not depart from God's great and long-promised Messiah. We will not forsake God's ultimate prophet who offers eternal life. We will not fail to give allegiance to our heavenly king."

Throughout John's Gospel, Jesus fulfills this prophetic role of not only representing God but also preaching God's revelation to the people. Consider how many times Jesus insists that his words come not from himself but from the Father (John 7:16; 8:26, 28, 40; 12:49–50; 14:24; 15:15). Even some of those who encountered Jesus recognized this reality and made such a confession (John 4:19; 6:14; 7:40; 9:17). Irrefutably, Jesus speaks the Word of God. In every single word of the Gospels, and in all of his teaching, he is a prophet; he is *the* prophet. In our most basic understanding, we recognize that in all Jesus did, in all Jesus said—in his person, in his display of acts, signs, and miracles, and in the events not only that he did but also those he explained—Christ reveals God and fulfills his prophetic office. Jesus reveals God in his person and work. Jesus does not fulfill the prophetic office as if he merely joins the ranks of another prophet among many. He comes as *the* prophet—the messianic and redeeming prophet—and thus Peter along with all of Jesus's disciples declare that they will not go away because Jesus has "the words of eternal life" (John 6:68). We hear them from no one else.

Chapter 5

The Messianic Prophet Fulfilled

The rest of the New Testament looks to the Old Testament in order to confirm Christ's identity as the prophet who would declare the way of salvation for mankind. The book of Acts twice cites the promise given to Israel in Deuteronomy 18. The first is the apostle Peter's sermon from Solomon's Portico:

> Therefore repent and turn back, so that your sins may be wiped out, that seasons of refreshing may come from the presence of the Lord, and that he may send Jesus, who has been appointed for you as the Messiah. Heaven must receive him until the time of the restoration of all things, which God spoke about through his holy prophets from the beginning. Moses said: The Lord your God will raise up for you a prophet like me from among your brothers.

> You must listen to everything he tells you. And everyone who does not listen to that prophet will be completely cut off from the people. (Acts 3:19–23)

Not only does Peter recognize Jesus as the appointed and anticipated Messiah, but he also proclaims that Jesus perfectly and completely fulfilled the promise of a messianic prophet. Firm apostolic authority demonstrates that the prophet God promised and to whom Moses pointed was none other than Christ Jesus himself.

A miraculous context precedes Peter's great declaration. Peter and John traveled up to the temple for the hour of prayer, and as they went, a lame beggar asked alms of Peter. Instead of giving the man money, however, Peter supernaturally restored strength to the lame man's ankles and feet in the name of Jesus (Acts 3:1–10). He performed a miracle both in like manner as Jesus had done and in Jesus's name. This miraculous working resembles the promise of Deuteronomy 34. No prophet like Moses had arisen in Israel since Moses. No one had come performing the degree of signs and wonders that the Lord sent Moses to do, and no one had done such mighty and powerful deeds before God's people and their enemies (Deut. 34:10–12). In its immediate context, Deuteronomy 34 makes reference to Moses, but taken in conjunction with Deuteronomy 18, it more significantly suggests the coming of another one who, though like Moses, would also stand apart as the ultimate and eternal prophet.

Without hesitation, Peter interprets Jesus Christ as the one who fulfills this expectation. From the moment that power goes out of him to heal the lame man, Peter turns to everyone looking on and announces that Jesus's "name—by faith in his name—has made this man strong whom you see and know, and the faith that is through Jesus has given the man this perfect health in the presence of you all" (Acts 3:16 ESV). Like Moses, the greater prophet would indeed perform signs and wonders. Peter says this miracle, which quickened the ankles and feet of the lame man, indicates the fulfillment of Deuteronomy 18. The Holy Spirit offers clear New Testament affirmation that Jesus fulfills Deuteronomy's expectation of the coming messianic prophet.

This testimony continues in Acts 7 as Stephen draws from Deuteronomy 18 to speak of Christ. Here, Stephen faces the same sort of drummed-up blasphemy charges as those issued against Jesus. Now, a religious council sits across from him trying him for these accusations and beckoning for his defense. Filled with the Holy Spirit (Acts 6:10; 7:55), Stephen replies and gives an account of Israel's history beginning with Abraham, Joseph, and then Moses. As he mentions Moses, he reminds his hearers that "this is the Moses who said to the Israelites: 'God will raise up for you a prophet like me from among your brothers'" (Acts 7:37). He cites Deuteronomy 18 and heralds the same messianic anticipation of the coming Prophet that Peter offered only several chapters earlier. On the authority of Moses, Stephen insists that another prophet like Moses would come. In a powerful concluding defense, he reveals in no uncertain terms that this prophet *did* come.

Stephen concluded his message by appealing to the prophets who foretold the coming Messiah. The inspired prophets after Moses "foretold the coming of the Righteous One, whose betrayers and murderers you have now become" (Acts 7:52). He recognized those standing in judgment over him as the authorities who only weeks ago put Christ to death. In his concluding words, Stephen connected the coming Righteous One with the prophet of Deuteronomy 18. Jesus Christ, he says, is this coming prophet. These texts from Acts offer Holy Spirit-inspired, apostolic authority affirming that Christ and his work fulfill the promise of Deuteronomy 18.

Chapter 6

Christ as Prophet Today

The three offices of Christ have not been finally fulfilled and closed, since we await the second coming of our Lord. Christians are saved and live in Jesus even now because of his continual work as Prophet, Priest, and King. Christ's prophetic office in particular gives us confidence because he represents us before the Father in heaven. The Dutch theologian Herman Bavinck describes Christ's current posture in this way:

> On the basis of the one, perfect sacrifice made on the cross, He now—in keeping with the will of the Father—distributes all His benefits. Those benefits are not the physical or magical aftereffect of His earthly life and death. It is the living and exalted Christ, seated at the right hand of God, who deliberately and with authority distributes all these benefits, gathers His elect, overcomes His enemies, and directs the history of the world toward the day of His

> parousia. He is still consistently at work in heaven as the mediator. He not only was but still is our chief prophet, our only high priest, and our eternal king. He is the same yesterday, today, and forever.[16]

With authority, Jesus declares the implications of God's Word for us. As Stephen takes his final breaths, Scripture describes Jesus's place in heaven through him in this way: "Look, I see the heavens opened and the Son of Man standing at the right hand of God!" (Acts 7:56). Christ's posture before the Father gives the Christian three assurances. First, we have assurance of our representation before God regarding our salvation. Our salvation comes not by our own merit; it is only through Christ's mediating work. Paul rejoices that "in him we have redemption through his blood, the forgiveness of our trespasses, according to the riches of his grace" (Eph. 1:7). Before God the Father, Christ speaks the truth of our reconciliation to God by the power of his sacrifice on the cross, a salvation accomplished through his Word. Christ is a proclaiming prophet on our behalf.

Second, Christians can be confident in Christ's Word as an agent of our sanctification. As we imitate Christ, we can look to his prophetic word as the means and guide to greater holiness. Referring to congregational worship, Paul described this Word's power in this way: "Let the word of Christ dwell richly among you, in all wisdom teaching and admonishing one another through psalms, hymns, and spiritual songs, singing to God with gratitude in your hearts. And whatever you do, in word or in deed, do everything in the name of the Lord Jesus, giving thanks to God the Father through him" (Col. 3:16–17). As will be demonstrated below, the local church is God's ordained setting for his Word to powerfully renew our hearts and minds.

Third, Christ's Word is a steadfast rock in the storms of life. Recounting a story about foundations of rock and sand during a storm at the end of the Sermon on the Mount, Jesus notes that "everyone who hears these words of mine and acts on them will be like a wise man who built his house on the rock. The rain fell, the rivers rose, and the winds blew and pounded that house. Yet it didn't collapse, because its foundation was on the rock" (Matt. 7:24–25). God's Word is a source of truth in a sinful world confused by falsehood. It is stability when everything else is shifting. Christians can be confident that they will face trials in the world, but they can also be sure in their faith in the Prophet. The messianic prophet's Word can guide them home. Because of these truths, Christians can live with confidence in the truth and power of God's Word in a world which is undergoing secularization with increasing velocity.

Chapter 7

Christ's Word and Our Salvation

Christ's prophetic office demonstrates three particular truths for believers: in relation to our salvation, to the local church, and to false prophets. Each of these will be discussed in turn. First, Christ and his words are the means of salvation found through personally hearing and receiving the gospel. The New Testament portrays Christ as the fulfillment of the messianic promise of redemption from sin which appears in Genesis 3: "I will put hostility between you and the woman, and between your offspring and her offspring. He will strike your head, and you will strike his heel" (v. 15).

The opening verses of the letter to the Hebrews make the case to Jewish readers that Christ, the messianic prophet, is greater than all preceding Old Testament messengers: "Long ago God spoke to your ancestors by the prophets at different times and in different ways. In these last days, he has spoken to us by his Son. God appointed him heir of all things and made the universe through him. The Son is the radiance of God's glory and the exact expression of his nature, sustaining all things by his powerful word" (Heb. 1:1–3).

Preceding Christ's incarnation, God's people heard his word through prophetic messengers. Christians living today have no need for such a prophet representing God and his Word. Christ, our Redeemer, has declared to us in himself our hope and grace.

John 1 makes this same assertion: "For the law was given through Moses; grace and truth came through Jesus Christ. No one has ever seen God. The one and only Son, who is himself God and is at the Father's side—he has revealed him" (John 1:17–18). God's Word—his revealed message of salvation—has come to earth. While the patriarchs of the Old Testament heard God's message and gave it to the people, Christ himself is both the communicator of the Word and the way of salvation himself. In John 14:6, Jesus makes this even more clear: "I am the way, the truth, and the life. No one comes to the Father except through me." The person and work of the Savior is the prophetic message of salvation to all mankind.

In keeping with the prophetic and declaratory nature of salvation, God uses means to bring unbelievers dead in sin to himself. For all Christians, there is someone who communicated the truth of the gospel to us. The apostle Paul expresses this principle in Romans 10.

> How, then, can they call on him they have not believed in? And how can they believe without hearing about him? And how can they hear without a preacher? And how can they preach

> unless they are sent? As it is written: How beautiful are the feet of those who bring good news. But not all obeyed the gospel. For Isaiah says, Lord, who has believed our message? So faith comes from what is heard, and what is heard comes through the message about Christ. But I ask, "Did they not hear?" Yes, they did:
>
> > Their voice has gone out to the whole earth,
> > and their words to the ends of the world.
>
> But I ask, "Did Israel not understand?" First, Moses said,
>
> > I will make you jealous
> > of those who are not a nation;
> > I will make you angry by a nation
> > that lacks understanding.
>
> And Isaiah says boldly,
>
> > I was found
> > by those who were not looking for me;
> > I revealed myself
> > to those who were not asking for me.
>
> But to Israel he says, All day long I have held out my hands to a disobedient and defiant people. (vv. 14–21)

As prophet, Christ brought and delivered the words of eternal life. Acting under the final prophet, Christians seek to share the gospel with all nations, knowing that the prophetic word they teach is the way of salvation. Just as Isaiah the prophet spoke to a disobedient world, Christians evangelize rebellious sinners separated from God by preaching the gospel to the nations.

Evangelicals sometimes truncate the Great Commission by failing to consider the implications of Christ's prophetic role for our daily lives and engagement with an increasingly secular world. Believers often rightly cite Jesus's declarations: "All authority has been given to me in heaven and on earth" (Matt. 28:18), and "Go, therefore, and make disciples of all nations, baptizing them in the name of the Father and of the Son and of the Holy Spirit" (Matt. 28:19). However, Jesus also affirms that this commission entails "teaching them to observe everything I have commanded you" (Matt. 28:20). Even now, Christ continues as prophet teaching his church through his word and teaching them to teach his teachings to others. Because of Christ, Christians stand prepared and ready to meet the contemporary moment with the power of his gospel message.

Jesus continues to speak to and teach his church in this way through the Holy Spirit. Jesus told the apostles of this promise in John 14, saying, "If you love me, you will keep my commandments. And I will ask the Father, and he will give you another Counselor to be with you forever. He is the Spirit of truth. The world is unable to receive him because it doesn't see him or know him. But you do know him, because he remains with you and will be in you" (vv. 15–17).

The distinction between those who follow Christ and those who do not is essentially one of prophetic words. The prophets and apostles have left a written record of God's Word in Scripture and are indwelt by the Holy Spirit, who guides us in our love for God and desire to follow these words. The Holy Spirit is present in us in this age as a teacher of Christ's words and commands. Jesus as the prophet continues to teach his church through the Holy Spirit, bringing to remembrance all that he has said.

Chapter 8

The Local Church: The Setting of Prophetic Action

Christ continues fulfilling his prophetic office in teaching his church through the written Word—the text of Scripture. In it, Christians find "the prophetic word more fully confirmed" (2 Pet. 1:19 ESV). The church continues Christ's prophetic work because it is founded upon Scripture, not human invention. Since the ministries of the church depend on biblical authority, they teach the church through the Word by the Spirit, who both brings to remembrance Jesus's words and teaches Christians all things. This is the heart of Christ's office as prophet, and it appears in many different aspects of church life.

Christ's role as prophet is most clear in the primary teaching setting of the local congregation, and it centers in expository preaching. As the pastor stands to declare and teach Scripture, he is explaining prophetic testimony. The most important task of any sermon must be seeing "what the Holy Spirit intends for your congregation" in a particular text of Scripture.[17] Expository preaching must be central to the life of any local church because it is the means by which God's Word is communicated and applied to us. Preaching is a fundamentally prophetic task. It is an expression of human dependance on God's revelation, not man's wisdom or other "prophecy."

The church's ordinances are also prophetic acts, declaring what is true about the Christian faith and the congregation's membership—namely, our salvation and covenant together. Local church membership is also a political act providing a prophetic witness before the world. Christians pronounce their faith in Christ through baptism, and they continually remember their salvation through the Lord's Supper. As one scholar has noted, the corporate nature of ordinances in Baptist churches lends them to a countercultural posture, serving as a revolutionary contrast to a self-centered modern world. "In baptism and the Eucharist, Christians declare their belief in the remarkable assertion that the "Word became flesh" (John 1:14), that he was baptized by John in the Jordan (Matthew 3:13–17; Mark 1:9–11; Luke 3:21–22), and that it is only by feeding on Jesus (John 6:35, 48) and his "words [that] are spirit" (John 6:53–63) that Christians receive eternal life."[18]

The prophetic Word is most clearly observable in the constituting and regular acts of faithful local churches, proclaiming the presently exilic and coming kingdom of God.

Chapter 9

Christ Against False Prophets

Christ's position as Prophet is an essential foundation for Christian ethics. In her 1953 short story "A Good Man Is Hard to Find," Flannery O'Connor describes the tragic tale of a roadside bandit known as the Misfit. The Misfit responds to self-righteousness in a woman he encounters, not with the Christian gospel, which he correctly identifies as total commitment to Christ, but with what he considers justice: murderous violence.[19] In a letter written nine years later, O'Connor describes the Misfit as "a spoiled prophet."[19] While she does not elaborate, it is possible that she is referring to his failure to face the almost humorous selfishness of man with the redemption revealed by God in Christ's prophetic office. He chooses his own prophecy and thus fails to provide any hope. Fulfilling a consistent theme in O'Connor's works, he fails to see the truth of God's revelation.

This failure is also a failure of our age, a time replete with spoiled prophets. They offer their own paths of redemption accomplished by their own ends. The public square is not only a battleground of truth claims; it is an acropolis of false prophets, all naming their own sins and offering their own forms of redemption. Christ's office as prophet is one of the most encouraging principles for Christians facing the confusing storm of secularization. His words are the truth about the human person and how God has designed us to live in this world.

The rapidly increasing velocity of cultural change on the issue of sexual ethics is one example of the difficulties with which Christians are presented. LGB quickly expands to LGBTQ+, and there is no indication of any respite for those who are convicted by the Bible's teachings. Thankfully, God's Word speaks prophetically about matters of sex and gender, male and female roles, marriage, and raising children "in the training and instruction of the Lord" (Eph. 6:4).

Making disciples requires hearing the Prophet's declarations, rejoicing to obey them, and teaching others to do the same—with infinite joy.

CHRIST AS

When I was a young boy, my grandmother gave me an annual subscription to *National Geographic* magazine. One of these volumes in particular was of special interest to me, as it surveyed the various world religions. From place to place around the globe, *National Geographic* would go in and research what a particular people ate, how they dressed, and how they behaved. They looked at what they believed and what their religion looked like.

If *National Geographic* observed anything in their study, it is that wherever you go, whatever the culture and religion, you invariably find priests. Of all the differences between the many religions, this seems to be a constant. Everywhere you look, you find priests because everywhere you look you find sons of Adam made in the image of God, unable to deny what we cannot help but know: that we are sinners who have wronged the God who made us and to whom we must give an account. Whether by adherents to Christianity[21] or to any number of pagan religions, the need for a priest is universally recognized.[22]

Chapter 10

The Roles of a Priest

In all these various religious systems, the job of the priest is largely the same. Most fundamentally, the priest's job is one of representation[23] and sacrifice.[24] For all the benefits of democracy in the modern West, our emphasis on political equality runs the risk of obscuring one reality that was recognized by all in the ancient world. The ancient peoples understood inherently that the common person had no right simply to approach a sovereign with any expectation of an audience. If this was true of the relationship between the people and a human sovereign, how much more must they have seen a need for a worthy representative to speak on their behalf to the gods? Thus, priests served to intercede for a people before a deity that the laity was otherwise unworthy to approach. This has been called the work of *intercession*: speaking, even making supplication, to the divine on behalf of others.[25]

But their unworthiness to approach the divine throne was not the only problem the ancients acknowledged with their relation to their deity. They recognized not only that they were unworthy to approach the throne but also that the lives they lived failed to meet the divine standards, and thus the wrath of the deity must be appeased. The priesthood served in this way as well, offering gifts and sacrifices to the gods in hopes of their favor and forgiveness. This has been called the work of *oblation*: the giving of gifts and sacrifices in order to appease divine wrath against human sin. The realization is basically universal where humans are found.

These two works seem everywhere to fall under the duties of the person called priest. Intercession and oblation are everywhere recognized as necessary—not just by the people of Israel but by all who are descended from Adam—because all who are descended from Adam are in need of a priest. *All* of humanity needs a priest.

Chapter 11

The Universality of Priests

That the office of priest is not unique to the Judeo-Christian religion is further evidenced by the reference to priests in the Bible even before the establishment of the nation of Israel and the Aaronic priesthood. Jethro, the father-in-law of Moses, was himself a Midianite priest (Exod. 3:1; 18:1). The Egyptians, too, had priests, such as Joseph's father-in-law Potiphera, called in Scripture the priest at On (Gen. 41:45). Still earlier we see in the biblical account Abraham, who had himself known only pagan religion before being called by the Lord away from Ur of the Chaldees. According to the Bible, the world was as full of priestly religions in Abraham's day as in the day of *National Geographic*'s. Everywhere Abraham looked in the land of Canaan, there too he saw the familiar presence of priests.

In the context of Abraham's sojourn, he encounters one of the most mysterious figures in all of Scripture, the priest

Melchizedek. We must turn back to Genesis 14 and the meeting of Abraham and Melchizedek. This is perhaps one of the strangest chapters in the entire Old Testament. Genesis 14:17–24 states,

> After Abram returned from defeating Chedorlaomer and the kings who were with him, the king of Sodom went out to meet him in the Shaveh Valley (that is, the King's Valley). Melchizedek, king of Salem, brought out bread and wine; he was a priest to God Most High. He blessed him and said:
>
> Abram is blessed by God Most High,
> Creator of heaven and earth,
> and blessed be God Most High
> who has handed over your enemies to you.
>
> And Abram gave him a tenth of everything.
>
> Then the king of Sodom said to Abram, "Give me the people, but take the possessions for yourself."
>
> But Abram said to the king of Sodom, "I have raised my hand in an oath to the LORD, God Most High, Creator of heaven and earth, that I will not take a thread or sandal strap or anything that belongs to you, so you can never say, 'I made Abram rich.' I will take nothing except what the servants have eaten. But as for the share of the men who came with me—Aner, Eshcol, and Mamre—they can take their share."

Does this passage make you yearn for Christ? It should, and it will if read properly.

At times the Old Testament can be confusing to believers. Not only confusing, but the apparent similarities to other religions can be used to claim that the Old Testament is somehow not trustworthy. But we know that the same Holy Spirit who inspired the Old Testament teaches us in the New Testament how to read the Old Testament. This is nowhere more true than in the book of Hebrews. When we read Genesis 14 (which admittedly is not the easiest passage to understand), we must rely on the guidance of the Holy Spirit. He is for us—not just an indwelling guide as we read the Scriptures; he is also the author of the divine commentary in Hebrews for how to read Genesis 14.

If the book of Hebrews teaches us anything about Melchizedek, it is that he serves in the Old Testament to foreshadow the Christ of the New Testament. In the priest Melchizedek, Christ is foreseen in psalms such as Psalm 110. Furthermore, he is the king of Salem, of Jerusalem. He is associated with Jerusalem, which is significant because, as the writer of the book of Hebrews tells us, it is Abraham who gives Melchizedek an offering (Heb. 7:4). Abraham treats Melchizedek as a *greater*, not a *lesser*. This is clear.

There is no explanation for Melchizedek except for a supernatural explanation. He is without father, without mother, and without ancestry. This is in stark contrast to Aaron and the Israelite priesthood that is descended from him, defined explicitly by ancestry, by patrilineal descent from the sons of Aaron. The only way you became a priest in the Aaronic priesthood was to be a male descendant of Aaron. But the Genesis text offers no explanation about where Melchizedek comes from. It's not descent. No mother, no father, no natural explanation. The figure of Melchizedek is shrouded in mystery, and this is intentionally so. But if we learn one thing from his role in the Old Testament, it is that there is precedent for a faithful priest of the Lord who is not of the sons of Aaron. The example of Melchizedek is amazing, but his main purpose is to point to Christ our prophet priest—our Great High Priest.

How is it that the various religions of the world all see the same office? The fact is, they did not create the office; they *recognized* it. That is, they recognized their need for it. The reason every religion has a priesthood is that every person needs what only a priesthood can offer: representation of the people to God through oblation and intercession. We are sinners and we know it. We know we need a priest.

Chapter 12

Israel and the Priesthood

What about the Aaronic priesthood of Israel? Exodus 28 and 29 describe the priesthood of Aaron and the duties given to it. What makes the priesthood in this account so interesting is how subtle the priesthood emerges in the context of the exodus.

As you read Exodus, you know that Moses has been speaking to, or serving as a prophet for, the children of Israel. The narrative goes on to describe the tabernacle in tremendous detail. In what may seem an extraordinary and elaborate description, the point is that the tabernacle is not a place of meeting between God and Israel based on the terms defined by Israel, at least in part. The entire context of the detail about the tabernacle is to make clear that in every respect, this is God's design for God's tent of meeting with his people. The extraordinary detail serves to reiterate this point beyond any chance of misunderstanding. The entirety of this work belongs to God. This is a sovereign act of God for Israel, and God is the sole designer. This is the tent in which he will meet with Israel. This is the tabernacle in which his presence will dwell.

But what is described after the tabernacle? The priests! The Lord continues to speak to Moses in Exodus 28:1–5 saying,

> Have your brother Aaron, with his sons, come to you from the Israelites to serve me as priest—Aaron, his sons Nadab and Abihu, Eleazar and Ithamar. Make holy garments for your brother Aaron, for glory and beauty. You are to instruct all the skilled artisans, whom I have filled with a spirit of wisdom, to make Aaron's garments for consecrating him to serve me as priest. These are the garments that they must make: a breastpiece, an ephod, a robe, a specially woven tunic, a turban, and a sash. They are to make holy garments for your brother Aaron and his sons so that they may serve me as priests. They should use gold; blue, purple, and scarlet yarn; and fine linen.

What follows in chapter 28 is an entire chapter of similar detail. Just as God personally, specifically, and intricately designed the tabernacle, so he also personally, specifically, and intricately designed the priestly garments.

Just as the details about the tabernacle sought to cause remembrance that the entirety of that work belonged to God, so too the intricate design of the priestly garments was meant to declare that the entirety of the workers and their work belonged to God. God is the sole designer of the place *where* he dwells and of the garments of the people through *whom* he mediates. These are the priests through whom he will relate with Israel. These are priests of the Most High, designed from on high.

These ornately adorned priests are men. This is a line of priests from the physical descent of Aaron. This is not an alien priesthood coming from outside of humanity. Even in small detail, the text gives insight to this end. Here, as is often the case in the Scriptures, the pronouns carry significant weight in rightly interpreting Scripture. The pronouns here are crucial. It is "Aaron, *your* brother" (Exod. 28:1, emphasis added), of whom God speaks to Moses. God is emphasizing the horizontal reality that exists between Moses and Aaron, highlighting that the priesthood God is initiating is a human priesthood. This is not a superhuman priesthood. This is not some kind of intermediary of anything other than human nature. It is just *your* brother, nothing less and certainly nothing more. In the present we too need another to mediate.

Now, remember, when examining the role of Christ as prophet, the promise that came from Deuteronomy 18 was that a prophet would arise from among you. So now in a similar way, even as the prophet emerged from among Israel, so also the priest emerges from among Israel. Consider the pronouns again: the priests will "serve *me*," says the Lord. Whom is the priest to serve? It turns out the priest is not primarily to serve humanity. Even though the function of the priesthood is to *represent* humanity before God, and the prophet *represented* God to the people by communicating the message of God, the priests were not going to serve themselves. The priests are to represent the people *before* God, but the priests do not *belong* to the people. These are not the people's priests. These are God's priests.

Let us turn our attention again to the priests and the priesthood. We see in Exodus 28:2 that God commands Moses, saying: "Make holy garments for your brother Aaron, for glory and beauty." This is interesting. Just think of the brothers Moses and Aaron. Think about the call of Moses and the emergence of Aaron. Think about Aaron's role as an adjunct to Moses. But Aaron's words are not determinative, important, or instrumental. It is the words of Moses that are determinative, important, and instrumental. But Moses describes himself as slow of speech (Exod. 4:10). In the exodus, the vocal cords of Aaron serve the message of Moses. But now in the priestly work, Moses has the responsibility to obey God by serving Aaron. God tells Moses, in the construction and preparation of these garments, you, Moses, shall make these garments for your brother Aaron (Exod. 28:2).

The garments are described as holy garments because this is a holy priesthood. The entire priestly responsibility is holy. There is no mistaking that the priesthood is a holy business, a holy ministry. These are specific holy garments, and we see why they are specified. But notice an interesting phrase about these garments in verse 2, where we read that these garments are to be made "for glory and beauty." This shows up again in the same chapter in verse 40. Why this particular detail?

It's difficult for the modern reader to imagine the context in which these instructions came from God through Moses to the people. What could be of importance in the color and form of the garments? Imagine walking through a great cathedral. Such a building is often beautiful, even breathtaking. When you enter a cathedral, you realize that this kind of beauty did not happen by accident. There is symmetry. There are intricate architectural schemes with massive stained-glass windows, which are reminiscent of the rose windows of the great medieval cathedrals. The walls are lined with dazzling color palettes, which blend many colors into stunning pictures. Just about everywhere you look, there is symmetry, form, and finish. Everywhere you walk, you are surrounded by color. You are surrounded by symmetry. You are surrounded by beauty.

In the wilderness Israel was surrounded by sand. Israel could see no artistry of scale. Now there were artisans, but the artisans had been serving Pharaoh. The artisans had no significant use of their skills in the desert, where they had been wandering for decades. What we must pay attention to in this transitional moment in Israel's history is that Israel is now going to be confronted with color. Life in Israel had been monochromatic until this point. But now, all the artistry, all of the beauty, and all of the aesthetics are going to be directed toward one focal reality: God's tabernacle. Whether it was the curtain that flowed in the wind or the hem of the priests' garments, all elements of the tabernacle boasted of a transcendent God who was immanent with his people, in this place, and with whom Israel could relate to through these men. All of it boasted of a transcendent God who was immanent with his people in this place whom Israel could relate to through these men.

The intricate instructions for the tabernacle include God's own delight in the colors he has made. You will notice that God mentions those to whom he has given particular skills, but God isn't asking these individuals to take creative liberties. God instructed them to use their artistry, but he is giving them an absolute pattern of what the minutest detail is supposed to look like, right down to where each border is supposed to be. God prescribes an exact length, an exact width, and an exact breadth of every dimension, right down to the location where the jewelry is to be placed.

It is important we remember in this the unity of the transcendentals. This is a basic theological principle. What do I mean by this? In the intersection of metaphysics and theology, one important principle is the unity of the transcendentals. The good, the beautiful, the true, and the real are the same thing. This is an important principle of biblical theology. God is one. God is indivisible. God is infinite in all his perfection. Yes, the good, the beautiful, and the true are good and beautiful and true and real. But because they belong to God, they are from God. God is the ultimate beauty, the ultimate good, the ultimate true, and the ultimate real, and all reflect God's nature. He is indivisible. So these qualities are indivisible. Even in our fallen state, we talk about truth and beauty as if we are talking about separate categories. The biblical worldview reminds us that what is true is also beautiful, and what is beautiful is also true. What is true is also good. What is good is also beautiful and true because the beautiful and the true are real.

You may ask, "What does this topic have to do with the priesthood?" The priests were to represent beauty, even in their garments. The garments were to be beautiful in and of themselves. But why were instructions for the aesthetic dimensions even necessary? Because we live in an aesthetically pleasing and colorful world, it is difficult for us to imagine their life in the wilderness. The only colors found in the middle of the sand were beige and brown! Everywhere you look, people are wearing the clothing of slaves who have escaped from Egypt. Now, in this tabernacle, there is going to be dazzling color. Men are being assigned as priests to the beautiful, true, and good God.

God intends to have truth, goodness, and beauty reflected in the priestly work. To that end, he designed a beautiful context from what the priests wear to the place where they would work. God, himself, has designated every *color* and formed every *pattern* and fitted every *jewel* in his grand design of the tabernacle and his priests who would work within.

God's artistry, reflected in his creation, was symbolized in the place where he would dwell with his people. The entire glory of God's creation is going to be demonstrated in the beauty and glory of these garments. Only the Creator, the God of the universe, would have priests like this. Out of the beige and bland, in that rugged desert, is a tabernacle adorned with stunning beauty and priests who wore beautiful garments made for glory.

Chapter 13

The High Priesthood

As we follow the history of the priesthood in Israel, we can notice three realities about priests. First, we understand not only that there are priests but also that there is an Aaronic priesthood. That is, the priests' succession is going to be defined by Aaron and his four sons. Second, we also come to understand that there will be a high priest, and the high priest is going to be the oldest male surviving of Aaron's line. And third, we discover the function of the Levitical priests.

At the beginning Exodus 28, we already have five priests—Aaron and his four sons. Much is about to happen, and we're going to have fewer than five in rather short order. But in verse 1, we have five priests, one of whom will be the high priest. This is the establishment of the Aaronic priesthood. There shall be from this point forward a priestly descent from Aaron's line.

Second, a priesthood not of many but of one. Israel will always have a high priest, the eldest male of Aaron's line. And yet, at the most crucial moments in the nation's history, Israel does not have a priesthood of many but a priesthood of one. In both the tabernacle and later in the temple, when on the Day of Atonement, a sacrifice is made inside the holy of holies, there is one priest. It is not a group of priests who approach but only one, the high priest (Lev. 16).

Now that's already pointing us to something. Even though there is a priesthood for the entire descent of the males of Aaron's line, the most crucial moment of atonement, the most crucial moment of each year, is a sacrifice by one single priest. It is not *priests* who perform this crucial ministry but a *priest*, one representative of the entire people. One high priest singularly bears the responsibility to enter the most holy place, and faithfully, lest he die and the people—by extension—with him. The priest must scrupulously fulfill what God has required of him.

Third, the Levitical priests. As we continue in the Old Testament there are other priests. There are the Levites, who are often misunderstood. It is right to describe them as those who help to prepare for the ministry of the Aaronic priesthood. They are the minor priests compared to the major priests. They are helpers, in a holy way, in a holy place. But that is not all they did. We come to learn from the prophet Malachi that the Levitical priesthood also bore the responsibility of teaching (Mal. 2:7). They also participated in the responsibility of representation, although not in quite the same way as the Aaronic priesthood (1 Chron. 23:28–32).

As we continue through the Pentateuch and as we see the development of the priesthood unfold, think about all that God has designed already and stipulated with the tabernacle and with the priestly garments. We see that everything has been made ready for this glorious and beautiful priesthood. But things quickly go awry. Aaron's great failure in making the golden calf serves as one example. Aaron is the one who is called with his four sons to begin the priesthood of Israel. Aaron is called to establish the Aaronic priesthood in truth, goodness, beauty, and reality. Aaron leads Israel during the absence of Moses, when Moses goes up to the mountain to be with the Lord. In Moses's absence and a claim of God's, Aaron devises his own priesthood—a priesthood whereby he serves not according to the will of God (Exod. 28) but according to the will of the people (Exod. 32:1–6), in the invention of a bovine idol—a golden calf. Now, this should tell us something that we should have seen all along. We should have known that as vitally important as it is to understand that God gave Israel the priesthood, the priesthood nevertheless collapses in human weakness and folly, just a handful of chapters after it was established.

It is not just Aaron who fails, however. Later, two of his sons also fail. Leviticus 10:1–3 reads,

> Aaron's sons Nadab and Abihu each took his own firepan, put fire in it, placed incense on it, and presented unauthorized fire before the LORD, which he had not commanded them to do. Then fire came from the LORD and consumed them, and they died before the LORD. Moses said to Aaron, "This is what the LORD has spoken:
>
> > I will demonstrate my holiness
> > to those who are near me,
> > and I will reveal my glory
> > before all the people."
>
> And Aaron remained silent.

Can you imagine a priesthood more disastrous than what is described here? Just a few chapters ago, there were five priests set apart by God with all the necessary preparations made for this Aaronic priesthood to continue in glory and beauty. This was even represented in the garments they would wear! God was not ashamed to call them "my priests." These are still God's priests. And yet the system is not looking good. Aaron himself turns into a pagan priest in the episode of the golden calf, and his two sons follow suit in their offering of the strange fire.

Remember how scrupulous God was about his stipulations. It is to be *all* according to his design, according to *his* standards. God included precise details about everything from the tabernacle to the garments and administrations of the priests. Yet here you have two of Aaron's sons bringing strange fire upon the altar. God's anger burned against the people as a result of their idolatry toward the golden calf (Exod. 32:7–14), and here in Leviticus 10, you see God pour his wrath upon these priests. God had warned the priests lest they die (Exod. 19:22). Now two of Aaron's sons are dead.

But this is not the end of the priests' unfaithfulness. If you have read and understood the flow of the Old Testament, you will remember that many other priests that follow will not get much better. It's a sad situation. The fate of the priesthood is without hope; the condition of the priest is without holiness; the priests are without fidelity. Infidelity plagues the priesthood. The lack of obedience is evident. Consider the prophetic condemnation of the priesthood in Malachi 2. Yes, there are certain priests such as Eli who demonstrate admirable characteristics, but again, his sons are a disaster (1 Sam. 1:22–25).

Upon seeing the priesthood God designed and established wallowing in such hopeless failure, we may rightly ask: "What is the point of all this? What is the point of establishing a priesthood simply to have it fail? What is the point of showing us priest after priest that fails to live up to his role?" The point is to make us yearn for a priest who will *not* fail. It is to make us yearn for a priesthood that fulfills the priestly duty. Furthermore, it should not be a yearning for a priest that will merely fulfill the priesthood in its old covenant duties. We should be yearning for a priest who is able to make *perfect* intercession and oblation.

Chapter 14

The Complexity, Multiplicity, and Insufficiency of the Sacrificial System

In considering the Old Testament teaching on the priesthood, we see that the complexity of the sacrificial system in Israel is astounding. There was meticulous detail for each sacrifice and often for repetitive sacrifices. By the time you come to Jesus cleansing the temple in the early chapters of the Gospel of John (2:13–16), we must remember Israel's population has grown. More people mean more sinners; more sinners mean even more sacrifices had to be made. Many sacrifices were required for many people every day. This was a lot to keep up with. It entailed a full-time vocation for many men at any given time. A cursory reading of the Pentateuch makes this much clear regarding the sacrificial system—it was complicated.

The Day of Atonement was itself the focal point of the sacrificial system. It was the high point of the Israelite year, but it had to be carried out every year. Once was not enough. Year after year, generation after generation, the need for atonement was constant under the old covenant. Just think of all the animals that were killed, the number of lives that were given, and all the blood that was spilled for the atonement of Israel's sin. But none of these sacrifices—not even all of them together—could fully atone for Israel's sin. That is why sacrifices had to be made over and over, again and again. There was no single sacrifice, just a recurring multiplicity.

Imagine all the high priests, generation after generation. Consider what they must have thought. They would have entered the most holy place on the Day of Atonement to fulfill the sacrifice, only to have it need to be done all over again because of Israel's continuing sin. Their work was complex; their sacrifices were many. And surely this toil would all have been a small price to pay–except that, in the end, it was insufficient. Granted, it was not for nothing that they did this. Their fulfillment of the covenant expectations secured for the people a flourishing life in the land promised to them. God's wrath was temporarily stayed. But in terms of the salvation they so desperately needed, the system was obviously and woefully insufficient. The blood of bulls and goats cannot save. This is a sad situation, but it is not without hope. The insufficiency of the sacrifices amid the multiplicity of their sins was the point. Where can sufficient atonement be found? That is where we now turn in the inauguration of the new covenant. The insufficiency of the priesthood of old pointed to a need for a greater high priest.

Chapter 15

New Covenant Priesthood

Christian theologians have not always agreed regarding how the Old Testament relates to the New Testament, and that is no less the case concerning the priesthood. However someone understands the relationship between the old and new covenants, it clearly entails both continuity and discontinuity.

On the one hand, much changes between the Old and New, for now the Messiah has come. All that foreshadowed him is now seen in vivid color. The author of Hebrews declares the old covenant to be obsolete now that a new covenant has been inaugurated in its stead (Heb. 8:13).

On the other hand, it is the same God at work bringing about the same demonstration of his same great glory, through the one gospel of salvation extended to Jews and Gentiles alike. As the apostle Paul writes to the church at Rome, his gospel is one of old mysteries revealed and of old prophecies fulfilled

(Rom. 16:25–26). The same truth is summarized in Augustine's famous maxim, "The New is hidden in the Old and the Old is revealed in the New."[26] The Old and New Testaments do not tell two different stories but the same story from different perspectives. Both bear witness to the gospel of Jesus Christ, the Old doing so in prospect and the New in its unfolding and in retrospect.

The old covenant was always intended to serve the purposes of the greater new covenant. While it promised the salvation that was to come, the old covenant was not itself a salvific covenant. The Mosaic system was never intended to save people everlastingly from their sins. It served to govern the nation God had established through the seed of Abraham through its system of laws. Through this it foreshadowed various aspects of the kingdom of Christ, such as the peculiar holiness of his people. Additionally, it preserved the lineage of Noah's son Shem, in whose tents the Gentiles were long since promised to dwell. Through the Semitic line the Messiah would be foreshadowed, would come, and would live in perfect obedience to the law—all revealed through the Mosaic covenant. Moses's covenant prepared the way for salvation, but Christ's covenant effected that salvation.

The Aaronic priesthood of the old covenant, therefore, was not salvific either. No part of the elaborate system of repeated sacrifices performed by the priests ever saved a soul. The sacrifices of the old covenant priests were sufficient to preserve the people's right standing before God, according to the terms of the old covenant. If it was done properly, they could continue living in the land promised to them, the land wherein God dwelled with them. The sacrifices of the old covenant priests were not, however, sufficient to atone for sin in such a way as to reconcile a sinful individual to a holy God.

There was always a distinction, therefore, between the nation of Israel, which consisted of all those who were descended from Jacob's twelve sons, and the true, spiritual Israel, which depended not on one's being descended from Abraham according to the flesh but according to faith (Rom. 9:6–7). Thus Rahab (Heb. 11:31), a Gentile convert not descended from Abraham, and David, a physical descendent of Judah, were both justified not by faith in the high priests of the old covenant but in the Great High Priest of the new covenant, Jesus Christ, whom all the others foreshadowed (Heb. 11:1–2).

Chapter 16

Christ as Priest

Priest is one of many titles attributed to Christ throughout Scripture. Some of those are implied figuratively, and others explicitly named. When Christ declares himself to be "the door of the sheep" in John 10:7 (ESV), he does not intend for us to understand him to be a construction of wood. Rather, we recognize the metaphorical similarity he draws between that through which the sheep enter the security of the flock and himself, through whom all must enter the kingdom of God. When we declare Christ to be priest, we intend no such similitude. Christ does not in some way *resemble* a particular characteristic of an old covenant priest. He *is* a priest—the Great High Priest—not figuratively but in reality. It is Christ whom all the nations need, as indicated by the ubiquitous semblances of a priesthood. It is Christ whom even the high priests of ancient Israel were designed to resemble and foreshadow. He does not bear a resemblance to them, but they to him.

Nowhere in the New Testament is the high priesthood of Christ more clearly expounded than in the book of Hebrews. Hebrews 4 has this to say about Christ's work as high priest: "Therefore, since we have a great high priest who has passed through the heavens—Jesus the Son of God—let us hold fast to our confession. For we do not have a high priest who is unable to sympathize with our weaknesses, but one who has been tempted in every way as we are, yet without sin. Therefore, let us approach the throne of grace with boldness, so that we may receive mercy and find grace to help us in time of need" (vv. 14–16).

The tremendous import of those first words must not be overlooked. "Since we have a great high priest" (Heb. 4:14). We do? Do not let those words pass over you. The words "since we have a great high priest" should cause us to exclaim, "Yes we do!" The author of the book of Hebrews also describes that Jesus has passed through the heavens. The Great High Priest, the Lord Jesus Christ, the incarnate Son of God, ascended into heaven.

On the basis of this sure truth, the author exhorts his Hebrew audience to "hold fast to our confession." Why? They were tempted to abandon it. For the Hebrew people, the Jewish faith—according to the old covenant—was familiar and comfortable. It was not only more convenient to adhere to the old covenant traditions, but the Jewish people were also already recognized and allowed to continue their religious practices under Roman rule.

Life was not so simple for Christians. People quickly became suspicious of what they saw as a new sect of the Jewish faith with sometimes radically different doctrinal claims and religious practices. On the one hand, they desired to confess the Galilean Jesus as the Great High Priest who had offered a once-for-all atonement for sins in his own death, risen from the grave, and ascended into heaven to make continual intercession on behalf of his people. On the other hand, wouldn't it be far easier to continue a historically tried and true system of men who made no grand claims but simply went on about the repetitive work of slaughtering animals on behalf of the people of God? After all, the Jewish priests too were ordained by God. The whole system of sacrifices was prescribed meticulously in Scripture by God through the prophet Moses. *What could be wrong with returning to something ordained by God?* thought the early Hebrew Christians.

But the old covenant priesthood had run its course. It had served its purpose, and it was made obsolete. It had been fulfilled in Christ. The confession is simple: Christ *alone* has served as the Great High Priest in offering up an atonement for sins. Christ *alone* can reconcile sinful man to the holy God. No other priest can fulfill this greatest need of all humanity. Either Christ is high priest, or no one is. Christ *alone* is able fully to do the work of a high priest, our Great High Priest.

Let's be clear about the Christology presented to us by the author of Hebrews. The confession to which we hold, the hope Scripture offers, is found in a proper understanding of the doctrine of Christ. The church has historically confessed that Christ is truly God and truly man. To this the author of Hebrews appeals, as he writes that in Christ "we do not have a high priest who is unable to sympathize with our weaknesses, but one who in every respect has been tempted as we are, yet without sin" (Heb. 4:15 ESV).

In the incarnation, the Second Person of the eternal Godhead assumed humanity, becoming human in every way. Let this sink in for a moment: Jesus is as human as you are. He lived a real life on this earth, experiencing the full breadth of human experience, including the real temptation to sin. And this, the author says, in every way. There is no manner of temptation Jesus has not faced in his humanity. Jesus knew what it was like to be tempted intimately. Yet despite all the innumerable times you and I have succumbed, he never did. Jesus withstood temptation every time.

But can he really appreciate the full weight of temptation without knowing firsthand the power it seems to wield in that pivotal moment of giving in? It may seem that he could not, but this could not be further from the truth. On the contrary, he knows more fully the weight of each temptation for the very reason that he has not given in where you and I have. The power it wielded in that moment that led you to break, he withstood, and the likelihood is that that was not the full force of the temptation's power. In withstanding temptation one appreciates how strong it is. C. S. Lewis explains memorably: "After all," he writes, "you find out the strength of the German army by fighting against it, not by giving in. You find out the strength of a wind by trying to walk against it, not by lying down. A man who gives into temptation after five minutes simply does not know what it would have been like an hour later."[27] But Jesus does. He knows because he has been tempted in every way and has withstood every time. He is human just as we are, and so he is able to sympathize with us in all our weaknesses.

Unlike any other priest of any other religion, however, this Jesus—who can sympathize with us in our weakness—is not only human but also holy, having withstood these countless temptations and perfectly kept the law of God, which we have broken.

We can, therefore, the author of Hebrews implores us, draw near to the heavenly throne with confidence. How could we not, with a high priest who so understands our human estate, having experienced it properly and in full? There is no manner of human experience to which Jesus cannot relate. Are you tempted? You can approach the throne with an advocate who was tempted for forty days (Matt. 4:1–11), even for more than thirty years. Are you overly busy? Jesus knows what it is to work indefatigably for years on end. Are you tested by a difficult acquaintance? Jesus traveled full-time with twelve of them. Are you enduring grief? Jesus knows what it is to weep over the death of a loved one (John 11:33–35) yet to rejoice in hope of the resurrection (John 11:23–25). In his humanity, Christ as high priest provides us bold access to the throne. A life lived with Christ as our priest is a life lived in prayer. A life lived with Christ as our priest, is a life going to his throne with confidence (Heb. 10:22).

One thing to notice about the book of Hebrews is that we have a better explanation of the Old Testament priesthood from this book than we do from the entire Old Testament! In the Old Testament, we must compile all kinds of texts together in order to get a comprehensive understanding of their identity, their function, and what impact their ministry had. And yet, all of that is explained in the book of Hebrews. The Holy Spirit, through the book of Hebrews, teaches us how to read the Old Testament, how to understand the Old Testament priesthood and the role of the high priest. In Hebrews 5:1 (ESV), we have a Holy Spirit-inspired summary of the old covenant duties, a brief, inerrant summary of the high priestly role. "For every high priest chosen from among men is appointed to act on behalf of men in relation to God, to offer gifts and sacrifices for sins." A priest is a priest. However, no sinful priest is able to fulfill these duties in their true and fullest senses, even the priests of Israel. Jesus alone can serve perfectly as high priest to God on behalf of humanity, and he is our sure high priest. But how? By becoming the necessary sacrifice and then by continually interceding for us.

First, Jesus offered himself as the once-for-all oblation to the Father, becoming at once the propitiation and the expiation necessary to effect our reconciliation with God. Jesus's sacrifice as the spotless Lamb of God must be understood in light of a long history of sacrifice throughout human civilization that we can trace back all the way to Adam and Eve. In the garden, no sooner than when sin entered the world did sacrifice graciously follow. Genesis 3 tells of the original sin of our first parents but also of the ensuing conversation between the participants and God, against whom they had sinned. Adam had sinned against the God with whom he had previously walked through the garden in friendship. Adam knew that he had brought upon himself the wages of that sin. He was no less clear as to what those wages were than we are now. God had told him plainly that the wages of sin is death (Gen. 2:17).

When confronted by God, then, Adam understood that if he was to escape the consequences of his action, he would need a sacrifice in his stead. The dissolution of horizontal friendship shared even between man and wife broke down almost immediately after the dissolution of Adam's vertical friendship with God, as he in his newly fallen state committed the reprehensible sin of attempting to sacrifice Eve by casting the blame on her (Gen. 3:12). Praise be to God, he had a different sacrifice in mind. Sparing both Adam and Eve the immediate death they expected, God slaughtered an innocent animal and clothed the sinners in its garments.

It is easy for us to look back on this first narrative and understand the clear foreshadowing of the Christ to come. For the many peoples throughout history who have not had the clear teachings of the Scriptures, the memory of the typological sacrifice made for our common parents manifests itself instead in a presumptuous preponderance of pagan priesthoods, one after another. With the clarity of the Scriptures, we understand that Christ is the spotless Lamb of God, the fulfillment of the desire of the nations—the perfect priest who appears offers a perfect sacrifice.

From the moment the eternal Son of God assumed humanity, he lived to die as a sacrifice that would satisfy the righteous wrath of God against sinners. This includes completing his life lived in perfect obedience to the law of God, which theologians have referred to as his *active* obedience. The death he died as an act of obedience on the cross has likewise been called his *passive* obedience.[28]

In life, Christ acquired for his people the righteousness of obedience required by the law. In death, he paid in full the penalty acquired by his people for their disobedience to the law. All of humanity must obey God perfectly. This is because God is perfect. The Jews would have heard time and time again—though they seem to have, like us, forgotten—"Be holy because I am holy" (Lev. 11:44). God's holiness is to be imaged in his image bearers. Yet who among us has fulfilled this calling? We have failed at every step of the way. We all turned away and became corrupt; none of us have done good (Ps. 14:3). Quoting this verse, Paul makes clear that Jews and Gentiles alike have sinned

(Rom. 3:10). Our sin is apparent through the law, and so is the reality that no one shall be right before God by obeying the law (Rom. 3:20). Not only that, but all of us are due the wages of our sin, that is death (Rom. 6:23). Yet Christ has secured the gift of God, eternal life, for us. He "humbled himself by becoming obedient to the point of death—even to death on a cross" (Phil. 2:8).

No other sacrifice could ever have accomplished what Christ did. It took the self-sacrifice of an eternal yet human high priest to offer on behalf of his people the necessary satisfaction of the wrath of God. All of this Christ did in the name of love for all who would but trust in him (1 John 4:10). Jesus's priestly work of sacrifice for sins is finished, just as he declared in his final words on the cross (John 19:30). The penalty is paid in full. It is finished.

The second way Jesus perfectly serves as our high priest is in his constant intercession for those who are his. His sacrifice is over, but his intercession can never end. The love of Christ in the gospel is put remarkably on display in all that has been discussed thus far, but we must add to all of this the incredible reminder of its permanence. What makes the incarnation of the eternal God all the more astounding is that it was never temporary. It is true, Jesus lived two millennia ago and was just as human as you are reading this now. But that is only part of the truth. He remains just as human as you are now but perfect and forevermore. The humanity and deity of Christ are both perfectly portrayed as the divine Son of God is seated at the Father's side, still sympathetic to our weaknesses, interceding for us.

What exactly is there to intercede for? For that matter, what does *intercession* mean? Outside of theological conversation, it is a word we don't often use. The word appears only a few other times in the New Testament, and each time it refers to the making of a supplication or petition to a person of authority. Christ's intercession is, in short, a prayer. In interceding for us, we mean that Christ is praying for us. But what possibly could he be praying for us?

We receive a glimpse of the answer to this question in John's Gospel. John 17 records for us what has long been called Jesus's high priestly prayer. It is called such because in it he so clearly intercedes to the Father on behalf of all who are his. Jesus is surrounded by his eleven disciples—since Judas Iscariot has already gone out to betray him—on the night before he was crucified. In prayer Christ lifts his eyes to heaven to ask four things for those whom he is about to leave behind in this world. At this point in the narrative, Jesus will soon die, be buried, resurrected, and ascend to be with the Father in heaven. In that day he desires that his disciples have four things.

First, he asks the Father to "keep them in your name" (John 17:11 ESV). That is, Jesus prayed for the security of those who are his, that they might not be lost to sin and temptation. Jesus was about to die on the cross to purchase this everlasting security, but he nevertheless demonstrates in this prayer the burden that was upon his heart. Prayer is no substitute for action, just as action is no substitute for prayer. Where there is sincerity, the two go hand in hand. As high priest, Jesus not only worked out salvation on the cross; he prayed for it as well.

Second, Jesus asks the Father for their salvific security to be manifested in earthly unity, "so that they may be one as we are one" (17:11). Just as the Father and Son are distinct persons, yet love one another perfectly throughout eternity, so Jesus came to share with us that great love. That great love is shown to us not only in our love for God but also toward one another. This benefit of his priesthood on our behalf is of course one of the clearest ways in which we manifest to the world that we belong to him—that we are beneficiaries of the love he has demonstrated as high priest. Just as on the cross he worked to accomplish the security for which he prayed, so also he broke down the dividing wall of hostility, that even the most disparate of believers might in him know this unity (Eph. 2:14).

Third, he longs that they may have his "joy completed in them" (John 17:13). The joy Jesus knows as the Son with the Father is the very joy Jesus wants us to have. Because Jesus wants us to share in that joy, he intercedes for us to that end. Praying to the father he says, "Now I am coming to you, and I speak these things in the world so that they may have my joy completed in them" (John 17:13). With this in view, he makes the next petition.

Fourth, he asks that they be sanctified, or made holy, according to God's truth (John 17:17). Throughout his time with the disciples, he had worked toward this end. As the great Prophet, Jesus lived among them as God's truth incarnate, teaching and admonishing them that they might be made more like him. As the Great High Priest, he intercedes on their behalf that this truth would change them. The relationship between these last two petitions is an important one. Jesus did not come to be a priest and bring about a holy people simply because it would be good for there to be more holy people. The disciples for whom he prayed that night could just as easily have been condemned for their lack of holiness rather than delivered from it. The three persons of the eternal Godhead would have been no less satisfied in themselves. No, Jesus's purpose was one of love. Jesus prayed that his joy would be completed in his disciples (John 17:13). This joy, however, did not come from being taken out of the world (John 17:15). Rather, Jesus prayed that while being protected (John 17:15) they would be made holy while in the world (John 17:17–19). He came to save us from our sins.

So, in his high priestly prayer, Christ intercedes before the Father, praying for his people that we might have security and unity, joy and holiness. And what's more, he prays this not only for those disciples who were there with him that evening "but also for those who believe in me through their word" (John 17:20). When we read John 17, we listen in on a prayer uttered for us. And we do so in confidence that not one of Jesus's prayers will ever go unanswered.

More amazing still is that the loving intercession offered on our behalf is continued by Jesus today, *even this very moment*. Paul exults upon this truth in Romans 8, anchoring our everlasting security and joy in the fact that "Christ Jesus is the one who died, but even more, has been raised; he also is at the right hand of God and intercedes for us" (Rom. 8:34). *Right now*, we who believe have an advocate with the Father (1 John 2:1). An advocate who sympathizes with us and who is interceding for us so that we might have security, unity, and joy in holiness—all thanks to the priesthood of Christ.

There is yet another way in which Jesus's priesthood is superior to that of old. Hebrews 5:2–3 says that a high priest "is able to deal gently with those who are ignorant and are going astray, since he is also clothed with weakness. Because of this, he must make an offering for his own sins as well as for the people" (Heb. 5:2–3). Take note of this: the high priest was to offer sacrifice for his *own* sins. Of course, this was implicit in the Old Testament, but it was not explicit. Remember, the high priest in the Old Testament was a human from among the people. The first was Aaron, brother of Moses, a sinner just like all the rest of Israel (Exod. 28). He was representational, but he was also a sinner. So, as the writer of the book of Hebrews makes clear, when the high priest performed the sacrifice on the Day of Atonement, he had to refer to his own sins as well as the sins of the people (Lev. 9:7; 16:6).

Of course, the high priest, who was of Aaronic descent, was human. Of course, that high priest could identify with other sinners because he was one. There was nothing unusual in the fact that Israel's high priests could identify with the sins and the temptations of the people because he himself was a sinner. When he performed the sacrifice, it was with reference to his own sin as well as to the sins of the people. But this is not so with our Great High Priest. That is the great distinction between *the Great* High Priest, and the other high priests. The final verses of Hebrews 4 clarify this, as the Great High Priest can sympathize with us in our weakness not because of his sin but precisely because he was "tempted in every way as we are, yet without sin" (Heb. 4:15). The comparison goes on when a few verses later the author says, "And no one takes this honor for himself, but only when called by God, just as Aaron was. So also Christ did not exalt himself to be made a high priest, but was appointed by him who said to him, 'You are my Son, today I have begotten you'" (Heb. 5:4–5 ESV).

Chapter 17

The Everlasting Order of Melchizedek

Returning to the priest Melchizedek, we can see now with greater clarity the way in which he served to prefigure Christ. Hebrews 5:7–10 (ESV) reads, "In the days of his flesh, Jesus offered up prayers and supplications, with loud cries and tears, to him who was able to save him from death, and he was heard because of his reverence. Although he was a son, he learned obedience through what he suffered. And being made perfect, he became the source of eternal salvation to all who obey him, being designated by God a high priest after the order of Melchizedek."

The only explanation for the high priestly ministry of Jesus is glory of divine sovereignty. The only explanation for Melchizedek is that he is from God. The only explanation for Jesus is the father's determination to save through his Son, and

Jesus is a high priest, after the order of Melchizedek. Concerning the order of Melchizedek, how does Jesus compare?

"Now if perfection came through the Levitical priesthood (for on the basis of it the people received the law), what further need was there for another priest to appear, said to be according to the order of Melchizedek and not according to the order of Aaron?" (Heb. 7:11). Jesus was like Melchizedek in that he did not become a priest on the merit of a legal requirement concerning bodily descent but by the power of an indestructible life. For it is said of Jesus that he is a priest forever, after the order of Melchizedek.

Christian, how hardheaded must we be for the Holy Spirit to have to repeat this so many times lest we miss it? Hebrews 7 a few verses later says, "None of this happened without an oath. For others became priests without an oath, but he became a priest with an oath made by the one who said to him: The Lord has sworn and will not change his mind, 'You are a priest forever'" (vv. 20–21).

Now we see why,

> Because of this oath, Jesus has also become the guarantee of a better covenant.
>
> Now many have become Levitical priests, since they are prevented by death from remaining in office. But because he remains forever, he holds his priesthood permanently. Therefore, he is able to save completely those who come to God through him, since he always lives to intercede for them.

> For this is the kind of high priest we need: holy, innocent, undefiled, separated from sinners, and exalted above the heavens. He doesn't need to offer sacrifices every day, as high priests do—first for their own sins, then for those of the people. He did this once for all time when he offered himself. For the law appoints as high priests men who are weak, but the promise of the oath, which came after the law, appoints a Son, who has been perfected forever. (Heb. 7:22–28)

Hebrews 8:6–7 sums this up wonderfully when it states, "But Jesus has now obtained a superior ministry, and to that degree he is the mediator of a better covenant, which has been established on better promises. For if that first covenant had been faultless, there would have been no occasion to look for a second one."

What happened on the cross was the offering, not by a high priest but by the Great High Priest. It was the Father providing the sacrifice he demanded for full atonement of sin because even though all the previous sacrifices held back God's wrath, they did not fully atone for sin. The atonement by Christ was "a propitiation by his blood" (Rom. 3:25 ESV). Now in the background is the necessary affirmation of a substitutionary atonement, a penal substitutionary atonement. This is an atonement in which the full penalty was paid for our sins as a propitiation God required and provided in Jesus Christ. We tend as evangelicals mostly to focus on the oblation of the sacrifice. Scripture reveals that Christ's priestly work is indeed oblation: sacrifice and atonement. But it is also intercession and mediation. And this is where we must remember that we are as dependent right now on the enduring, continuing mediatorial work of Christ as we were when Christ was on the cross. Understanding Christ's office of priest should cause us to be awestruck at the sheer mercy of God and his glorious work of redemption through Christ. Far too many Christians never come face-to-face with that glorious truth.

I began this section with a simple yet crucial statement: we need a priest. We desperately need a priest. It's true. *National Geographic* had that much right. Wherever you look around and see humanity, you see priests. Evangelicals are often prone to error on this point. Isn't the priesthood part of what we as Protestants protested against? We protested then, as we must do now, any corruption of the biblical doctrine of the priesthood. But we must with the same zeal cling eagerly to what the Bible does teach on the matter. Why? Because we do have a priest, a Great High Priest, in Christ. And because of his all-sufficient work, we need no other priest. There *is* no other true priest. Martin Luther was offended first and foremost by the abuses of the priesthood within the Roman Catholic Church. It was not long until the biblical and theological logic of the Reformation led him to understand the problem wasn't the abuse of the priesthood; the problem was the system of the Roman priesthood itself!

Thus, the gospel as revealed in Scripture led Luther to understand that what takes place in the Roman Catholic Mass is not a continuation of the sacrificial ministry, the atoning ministry of Christ. It's a *repudiation* of his ministry because Christ, the Great High Priest, died once and for all in full payment for our sins. As John Murray has written, "What the New Testament stresses is the historical once-for-allness of the sacrifice that expiated guilt and reconciled to God."[29] The acts of the Roman Catholic Church thus seemed to be slander against the actual atonement of the Great High Priest and the sacramental claims of the priesthood.

The evangelical instinct is perhaps to say we do not need priests interceding for us, and this is true. But we desperately need a priest, the one priest who has made a final oblation as a sacrifice for our sin and one who makes continual intercession in our interest. Rejoice, Christian, because we have such a priest. He is after the order of Melchizedek. He is the Great High Priest. Let us remember those beautiful words we love to sing,

> Jesus paid it all,
> All to Him I owe;
> Sin had left its crimson stain,
> He washed it white as snow.[30]

From the beginning of sinful humanity, we needed a priest. We at this very moment need a priest. We have such a priest. His name is Jesus Christ, our Lord.

CHRIST AS

What does it mean for us that Christ is King? As we read the Scriptures, we discover Christ clearly operating as Prophet. For when he talks, the words of God are spoken. We also see Christ operating as Priest. For he gave himself up as the perfect sacrifice for his people. However, while on earth, we never really see Christ operate as King in the way humans would expect a king to operate. Yet he was our King then, is ruling as our King now, and will hold this position throughout eternity.

Chapter 18

Kingship and the People of God

It is important to start with an understanding of kingship in the history of the people of God. Kingship has been an issue of some complexity and controversary among God's people since the formation of the nation of Israel. The cornerstone text in the study of "king" in all of Scripture is Deuteronomy 17. Moses writes in verses 14–20:

> When you enter the land the Lord your God is giving you, take possession of it, live in it, and say, "I will set a king over me like all the nations around me," you are to appoint over you the king the Lord your God chooses. Appoint a king from your brothers. You are not to set a foreigner over you, or one who is not of your people. However, he must not acquire many horses for himself or send the people back to

> Egypt to acquire many horses, for the LORD has told you, "You are never to go back that way again." He must not acquire many wives for himself so that his heart won't go astray. He must not acquire very large amounts of silver and gold for himself. When he is seated on his royal throne, he is to write a copy of this instruction for himself on a scroll in the presence of the Levitical priests. It is to remain with him, and he is to read from it all the days of his life, so that he may learn to fear the LORD his God, to observe all the words of this instruction, and to do these statutes. Then his heart will not be exalted above his countrymen, he will not turn from this command to the right or the left, and he and his sons will continue reigning many years in Israel.

Even though Israel will one day have a king, the context for this writing is that Israel does not yet have a king. God, in his infinite wisdom, speaks through Moses to inform Israel that one day they will demand a king. This passage does not recommend a king. Verse 14 describes the Jews' motivation for demanding a king: "When you enter the land the LORD your God is giving you, take possession of it, live in it, and say, 'I will set a king over me like all the nations around me'" (Deut. 17:14). The Jews desire a king so they can be like other nations. Their logic is that real nations have kings, thrones, and royal palaces. Their desires are not informed by God's desire. Their eyes are set upon creation rather than the Creator. So they dare to ask their perfect King for a human king.

The present-day reader would be justified to question why Israel feels incomplete. After all, the Lord God himself is the one leading the nation of Israel. How could a nation founded upon and led by the sovereign Lord of the universe demand a king? From this passage the nature of the human heart is seen. Humans seek an imperfect king but expect that king to lead them perfectly. They long for satisfaction but place their desires for fulfillment in all the wrong places and seek them with all the wrong means. God knows this about his creatures. After all, he was the one to put this longing for a king in human hearts. However, sin has corrupted this desire so that man is constantly looking away from the perfect King.

God in his grace sets limitations on the future human king of Israel. In ancient Near Eastern culture, to have a king was to have a totalitarian autocrat without any curbs on monarchial power. Israel's stubborn demands for a king will get them a king. However, the Lord's kindness ensures that the king of Israel will never be like the kings they thought they admired. The ancient Near East was full of kings who claimed to be a god-king. Any amount of studying the governments run by kings who thought themselves god-men shows how exploitive and autocratic these men were. There are constitutional and theological limitations upon Israel's king that will not be upon any other king. This is not God punishing whomever the king may be. The limitations are for the benefit of the people of Israel. The authority of Israel's king was not to be derived from a source of self but from an authority from God. Even when God relents and gives Israel over to their wrongful desires, he still seeks their betterment.

The king of Israel will be a king unto the one true God and not a totalitarian tyrant.

The Israelites wanted a king like the other nations, but their king is not to be like the kings of other nations. They get a king, but he shall be one whose authority is derived. It is a king whose kingdom has been established by the Lord. His reign shall only be so long as the lord sees fit. All kings are under the sovereign authority of the Lord, but this king will not be given any hint in his office that he serves anyone but the one true God. His power, authority, and dominion are not expressed from within but determined from without. Ultimately, Israel is not to receive a king like the nations at all. They were never meant to be like the other nations then, now, or ever.

The role that only Christ can fill is obvious. Israel will one day have the king they have been yearning for. He will rule with a mighty scepter and will hold the nations in his hand. He will have an authority given to him by God as the Son of God and will rule with all the authority of God, seated on the throne of glory.

First Samuel 8 records the demand of a king come to fruition: "When Samuel grew old, he appointed his sons as judges over Israel. His firstborn son's name was Joel and his second was Abijah. They were judges in Beer-sheba. However, his sons did not walk in his ways—they turned toward dishonest profit, took bribes, and perverted justice. So all the elders of Israel gathered together and went to Samuel at Ramah. They said to him, 'Look, you are old, and your sons do not walk in your ways. Therefore, appoint a king to judge us the same as all the other nations have'" (vv. 1–5).

Israel desired to be like the nations. They refused to see their special and unique constitution as a nation lead by Yahweh himself. Notice that Israel provides a unified front, gathering all the elders together. Israel's desire for new leadership is not what is wrong. We see in verse 3 that Samuel's sons "did not walk in his ways—they turned toward dishonest profit, took bribes, and perverted justice" (1 Sam. 8:3) The Jews saw Joel and Abijah as unfit for the role of judge over Israel, and they were right. Who can hold the role of judge and be themselves characterized by a perversion of it? Surely not one judging on behalf of God.

But will a king like the nations have resolve such injustice? As David Tsumura makes clear, their demands will not bring a solution to the problem they face. A king like that of other nations will bring neither stable leadership nor moral uprightness. A hereditary succession of leadership will not resolve their leadership foils, for "Samuel had already established it by appointing his sons as judges."[31] And as we have just seen, those appointed within the hereditary succession were fulfilling only the role of an unjust judge. They found neither stable leadership nor moral uprightness. Redefining the role of the one who sits on the seat will not guarantee that a stable or righteous moral man sits up on it.

Look carefully at this passage:

> When they said, "Give us a king to judge us," Samuel considered their demand wrong, so he prayed to the LORD. But the LORD told him, "Listen to the people and everything they say to you. They have not rejected you; they have rejected me as their king. They are doing the

> same thing to you that they have done to me, since the day I brought them out of Egypt until this day, abandoning me and worshiping other gods. Listen to them, but solemnly warn them and tell them about the customary rights of the king who will reign over them." (1 Sam. 8:6–9)

As surprising as the agreement is, what is clear from the Lord's response is that the people of Israel are not rejecting Samuel. By demanding a king, they are ultimately rejecting the Lord. In fact, this is not Israel's first demand for a king. Just like Gideon in Judges 8 and Jotham in Judges 9, Samuel does not relent. The people's demands make clear they are trying to supplant God. They are rejecting his desires and will for Israel. Robert Bergen suggests that the Lord is writing the thesis of Israel's history here in verse 8: forsake Yahweh, worship idols. "Against this backdrop, Israel's demand for an earthly king is presented as merely the latest instance of their long-standing pattern of rejection."[32] Time and time again, Israel rejects the herald of the King. This reveals their hardness of heart. They forsake God and worship idols. Present-day readers must pay close attention to their own souls that they never allow confidence in things of this earth to create a spirit of stubbornness and disobedience of God like is seen in the stiff-necked Israelites.

The Lord listens to their demands for a king and also retains his unquestionable and unconditional sovereignty in the process. There is no reality where Israel could truly usurp the Lord, even if it appears like they are about to do just that. As John Piper writes in his magisterial work on God's providence, the Israelites had God as their king, and they committed treason against him.[33] This people deserve to be blotted off the face of the earth for their iniquitous rebellion against the King, but Yahweh is gracious. As Piper shows reflecting on 1 Samuel 12:22, "God's commitment to the glory of his name is the ground of his gracious commitment to his people—and their king."[34] God still rules and reigns over this people and ultimately, he will determine who this king is:

> Samuel told all the Lord's words to the people who were asking him for a king. He said, "These are the rights of the king who will reign over you: He will take your sons and put them to his use in his chariots, on his horses, or running in front of his chariots. He can appoint them for his use as commanders of thousands or commanders of fifties, to plow his ground and reap his harvest, or to make his weapons of war and the equipment for his chariots. He can take your daughters to become perfumers, cooks, and bakers. He can take your best fields, vineyards, and olive orchards and give them to his servants. He can take a tenth of your grain and your vineyards and give them to his officials and servants. He can take your male servants, your female servants, your best cattle, and your donkeys and use them for his work. He can take a tenth of your flocks, and you yourselves can become his servants. When that day comes, you will cry out because of the king you've chosen for yourselves, but the Lord won't answer you on that day." (1 Sam. 8:10–18)

In giving a king to Israel, he is also giving them over to the responsibilities that come with having a king. This king will take their land and the best part of it. He will take their crops and the best of them. He will even take their sons and daughters from them.

Yet the most astounding thing written in this account is the resolute hard-heartedness of Israel: "The people refused to listen to Samuel. 'No!' they said. 'We must have a king over us. Then we'll be like all the other nations: our king will judge us, go out before us, and fight our battles'" (1 Sam. 8:19–20).

If we look back to what has happened prior in 1 Samuel, God has promised to do all that Israel is looking for in a king. He would judge them; he would even go before them and lead them into battle. But Israel rejected God as their king and decided still that this human king—who will ultimately fall short—is better suited for them. They demand a king they can see, even if the king would fail them.

Chapter 19

The Ideal King

When tracing the Old Testament history of the kings of Israel, you encounter an ebb and flow in the succession of Israel's kings. Israel's first king becomes the antitype of all kings. If there ever was a king that looked like a king, it was Saul. As a man, he was head and shoulders above all the others. Central casting would have had an easy choice when looking for the king of Israel. Saul looks like a king and fights like a king, and when Israel had Saul, they thought they had the ideal king. He entirely looked the part.

Yet Saul becomes a picture of Lord Acton's famous warning: "Power tends to corrupt, and absolute power corrupts absolutely."[35] As the Scripture unfolds, we discover not only the collapse of Saul as a king but the collapse of Saul as a man. Saul provided Shakespeare the model of King Lear, a king who simply dissolves while in authority. A character that completely dissolves in dissipation, with his kingdom at the mercy of his meltdown.

Saul becomes the antitype, which unfortunately became a predictable pattern when looking at an overview of the Old Testament monarchy. Yes, you have grand kings like Asa, Jehoshaphat, Uzziah, and Hezekiah. Yet the norm more commonly followed the model of evil kings like Ahaz, Manasseh, Amon, and Jehoiakim.

One day I was crossing the campus at Southern Seminary, and I saw a young man I knew was about to become a father. I asked him how things were going, and he said they had just had the ultrasound, and they learned they were going to have a son. I shared his obvious joy and then I asked him what he and his wife were going to name their son. He said they really wanted to name him after one of Israel's good kings. And I thought, that is a rather limited list. There are not many kings of Israel or of Judah after whom you would want to name a son. There are just not that many kings whose reign was characterized by faithfulness. Instead, too often their reigns are characterized by corruption, greed, and malice. Hard to find many good names.

Saul's direct successor becomes the ideal type of king, as far as a human king can be. David becomes the realization of Israel's greatness. David becomes the great warrior on behalf of Israel. We discover that "Saul has killed his thousands, but David his tens of thousands" (1 Sam. 18:7).

The temple is traceable to David, and in Israel's history it is remembered as a part of David's legacy too. Even though he was not allowed to build the temple, his son Solomon was. Solomon's reign was understood to be an extension of David's reign. There were glorious times and great achievements in Solomon's kingdom. Solomon's successes became so famous that he caught the attention and admiration of a foreign monarchy. Other kings and monarchs wanted to see the glory of Israel amid Solomon's reign.

Why was David perceived as the ideal king of Israel? The Bible is clear about David as a man and even about David as a sinner. Even as there is glory in David, there is humiliation in David and in his great sin. It is not as if Scripture records David committing some minor offense. The Bible makes David's sin abundantly clear in all of its undeniable horror. David's sin amounts to an orchestrated murder as a cover for his adultery. How glorious can a kingly reign be if the king is an adulterous murderer? And how can this same king be described as a man after God's own heart? It may not be possible this side of glory to have an adequate estimation of David. It is difficult to fully understand David at a distance. It is difficult to fully understand what God is revealing in and through David and in and through the Davidic monarchy, but Christ will rule forever from David's throne.

Remember that God made a covenant with David. This was a seismically important covenant that came with the promise that the throne of David will endure *forever*: "But that night the word of the Lord came to Nathan: 'Go to my servant David and say, "This is what the Lord says: Are you to build me a house to dwell in? From the time I brought the Israelites out of Egypt until today I have not dwelt in a house; instead, I have been moving around with a tent as my dwelling"'" (2 Sam. 7:4–6).

Notice God speaks of what he is not going to allow David to do. David is not to build a temple, which is David's clear intention in the verses prior. God is not going to allow David to build a temple to the Lord, but God will show that the coming covenant he will make with David is unconditional. David will not in any way earn the established position of king progenitor in a line of kings, establishing an everlasting kingdom of the Lord. The covenant itself is found within 2 Samuel 7:16–17: "'Your house and kingdom will endure before me forever, and your throne will be established forever.' Nathan reported all these words and this entire vision to David."

Nathan communicates to David that he will not be allowed to build the temple, but his throne will be established forever. That promise is breathtaking. In 1 Chronicles 17, this same truth is repeated in a more precise form:

> "When your time comes to be with your ancestors, I will raise up after you your descendant, who is one of your own sons, and I will establish his kingdom. He is the one who will build a house for me, and I will establish his throne forever. I will be his father, and he will be my son. I will not remove my faithful love from him as I removed it from the one who was before you. I will appoint him over my house and my kingdom forever, and his throne will be established forever."
>
> Nathan reported all these words and this entire vision to David. (vv. 11–15)

God's plan is for David's son Solomon to build him a temple, yet the fulfillment of this covenant is not expected to lie with Solomon. The words of this covenant point directly to Christ, the only Son of David who will not fail in being faithful to all of God's requirements. The fulfillment of God's promises to David was not Solomon but Christ.

Israel was given prophets to be the mouthpiece of the Lord, but the prophet that was promised to one day be like Moses had not yet come. There is an established priesthood, but this priesthood was incomplete, leaving mankind yearning for a perfect priest, a perfect Great High Priest. One who will not have to make sacrifice for his own sin, one who will make atonement in full for sin.

So, too, through the flow of biblical history, God's people yearn for a king—a king greater than David. In Israel's imagination they really could not even imagine a king greater than David, but they have been told they are looking for a king infinitely greater than David. As great as David was as king, he was not perfect. The rule and reign of David had one glaring issue, and it goes beyond David's sin with Bathsheba. The biggest issue with David's rule as king is he eventually dies. Israel had a great king, but all too soon Israel had a dead king.

This king, a man after God's own heart, was still an imperfect king. Even with David on the throne, we have an imperfect picture of the kingdom which is to cause us to yearn for another kingdom: the kingdom of God, the kingdom of Christ. We yearn for a different kind of king: a king whose rule was not compromised by human sin. A king whose rule was not limited by the inherit limitations upon a human sovereign—*a king who will not die*. A king who will rule and reign forever. A king whose reign will be perfect in the execution of justice and righteousness. A king whose reign will be accompanied with unwavering flourishing for his people. Israel yearned for that king and for that king to come. He did come and his name is Jesus.

Israel's problem was that its yearnings were directed toward the wrong kind of king, the wrong kind of ruler, the wrong kind of greatness. Their yearnings were not wrong. But their yearnings often caused them to look back to David rather than forward to God's covenant promise. The people of God would often ask for something like they had seen before instead of something they had not yet seen. Rather than their yearnings finding their end in God's kingdom, they set them in a kingdom just like the other nations.

There is a temptation in all of us that our yearnings would lead us somewhere in the past. That we might desire to go back to David or a time like his. But there is no going back to David. Ultimately, going back to David would just produce another David, who then would also sin and die. The Lord in his grace and sovereignty, knowing our human hearts, gives us promises of one infinitely greater than David:

> For a child will be born for us,
> a son will be given to us, and the government
> will be on his shoulders.
> He will be named
> Wonderful Counselor, Mighty God,
> Eternal Father, Prince of Peace.
> The dominion will be vast,
> and its prosperity will never end.
> He will reign on the throne of David
> and over his kingdom,
> to establish and sustain it
> with justice and righteousness from now on and
> forever.
> The zeal of the Lord of Armies will accomplish
> this. (Isa. 9:6–7)

Chapter 20

The King Foretold

An entire century of biblical scholarship tried to teach us that Isaiah 9 cannot be about Jesus. They claim this can only be the work of a proximate prophecy, with someone near to Israel. This seems preposterous because even if there had been some proximate fulfillment, it could not have been anything close to the actual, total fulfillment. There is no proximate human king who ruled forever. Look around. Where is he? This is a fool's errand. The only reason one would deny this prophecy is about Christ is if you deny the ability of a sovereign God to orchestrate creation to his great purposes. Isaiah says later:

> Then a shoot will grow from the stump of Jesse,
> and a branch from his roots will bear fruit.
> The Spirit of the Lord will rest on him—
> a Spirit of wisdom and understanding,
> a Spirit of counsel and strength,
> a Spirit of knowledge and of the fear of the
>   Lord.
> His delight will be in the fear of the Lord.

He will not judge
by what he sees with his eyes,
he will not execute justice
by what he hears with his ears,
but he will judge the poor righteously
and execute justice for the oppressed of the land.
He will strike the land
with a scepter from his mouth,
and he will kill the wicked
with a command from his lips.
Righteousness will be a belt around his hips;
faithfulness will be a belt around his waist.

The wolf will dwell with the lamb,
and the leopard will lie down with the goat.
The calf, the young lion, and the fattened calf
 will be together,
and a child will lead them.
The cow and the bear will graze,
their young ones will lie down together,
and the lion will eat straw like cattle.
An infant will play beside the cobra's pit,
and a toddler will put his hand into a snake's
 den. (Isa. 11:1–8)

The righteous reign that has been promised is more fully understood as we look at Isaiah 11. Have you ever wondered before where mankind came up with the concept of a king's reign? Did Israel's understanding of kingship and monarchy and rule and reign come only by the observation of the nations? Is it attributable only to the observation of Pharaoh and Egypt? Is it solely from their experiences of the various kings in all the vassal states and cities that dotted the landscape? Is that where the desire of kingship comes from?

Biblical theology makes clear that the idea of reign and the desire for a king was not something that was just observed by the people of God and then desired. It has been front and center in the entire trajectory of mankind. It comes from being made in the image of God by the one sovereign Creator. We hunger for a perfect king and his magnificent rule.

This Creator is God, the one who has exercised and forever will exercise his reign comprehensively and totally without condition or limitation. And he has placed within the hearts of his human creatures a yearning for righteous rule. A yearning for things to be made right.

Why do young children tend immediately to look for authority structures? How can you explain why leadership emerges? Is that just a sociological development? Is that simply power structures inherent to the stronger in an effort to suppress the weak? How come everywhere you look there is a king, yet everywhere you look such leadership is different from Isaiah's vision? If you are an evolutionist, in order to stay consistent, you must explain everything simply in terms of the mechanisms of evolution. If you are a naturalist or materialist, you have to explain everything simply in naturalism and in materialism. Those are the only terms available so a naturalist must explain how the world is produced through evolution and social development. But children look at the world and know there was some agent behind the existence of everything. Someone built our house, someone built our car, someone made dinner, someone must have made the world. Secularists now must solve the quandary of how a system of evolution can program people not to believe in evolution. That worldview also fails to explain why we yearn for a heavenly kingdom and a perfect King.

Biblical theology helps us look at Scripture and come to understand that God made us in his image and that yearning for authority, yearning for righteous rule, yearning for someone who has the power, the agency, the authority to make things right is a part of what it means to be made in God's image. Our Creator made us to look for a king!

So mankind has always known this yearning for a king. Much of human history has shown this yearning for a king has often been misdirected by sinful, fallen men. Our yearning for a king throughout history matches the yearning of Israel for a king. They waited and waited for the promised king to come, only to be disappointed by a myriad of earthly kings, all of whom eventually died. We now must turn to the New Testament to understand just how immediately Jesus is recognized as king when he appears on the scene.

Chapter 21

The Long-Awaited King

In the sixth month, the angel Gabriel was sent by God to a town in Galilee called Nazareth, to a virgin engaged to a man named Joseph, of the house of David. The virgin's name was Mary. And the angel came to her and said, "Greetings, favored woman! The Lord is with you." But she was deeply troubled by this statement, wondering what kind of greeting this could be. Then the angel told her, "Do not be afraid, Mary, for you have found favor with God. Now listen: You will conceive and give birth to a son, and you will name him Jesus. He will be great and will be called the Son of the Most High, and the Lord God will give him the throne of his father David. He will reign over the house of Jacob forever, and his kingdom will have no end." (Luke 1:26–33)

The reader of the New Testament does not have to search for the connection of the promise of Israel's long-awaited king and the fulfillment found in Jesus. Through the Holy Spirit, the people of God are given the words of Gabriel addressed to Mary—some of the most beautiful language in all of the Scriptures. Jesus—before he was conceived in the womb—is identified as the one to whom the Lord God will give the throne of David. Jesus is the fulfillment of the promise for a king of Israel to rule forever. The birth of this Son of David is the threshold of the fulfillment all mankind has been waiting for. This baby conceived within Mary will reign over the house of Jacob forever, and his kingdom will never end.

Matthew's account also records, as a consequence of Jesus's birth, the announcement of Christ's kingship: "After Jesus was born in Bethlehem of Judea in the days of King Herod, wise men from the east arrived in Jerusalem, saying, 'Where is he who has been born king of the Jews? For we saw his star at its rising and have come to worship him'" (Matt. 2:1–2). One of the main themes prevalent in Matthew's account is how the Gospel highlights the entire story of Jesus as the one who fulfills the promises the Jewish people have waited for—and for so long.

Consider therefore that Israel's promised great King did not arrive on the scene with royal fanfare. He did not arrive with an army. There were no harpists, no chorists, no throne. Christ did not arrive in Bethlehem and then lead an army to conquer Rome. No, Christ Jesus arrived as a baby. The King of kings and Lord of lords arrived in humility and was laid in a manger. Israel's long-promised king came as an infant, but he was announced by angels and witnesses by both shepherds and wise men. The King had come!

Remember King Saul and why he was anointed king? He looked like a king, acted like a king, and yet he turned out to be unfit for the role of king of Israel. Jesus's anointing is much the opposite of Saul's. He is anointed king as a baby with—as far as mankind can see—no reason to sit on this promised throne. However, the perfect king came at the perfect time to accomplish his perfect work.

This king—Christ the King—is not a king like nations have but King over all the nations. And the nations shall bring him gifts. The wise men come from the east for they have seen the star announcing the birth of the King.

When Christ came, he was not born a god-king as in the nations. He was born the God-Man in humility. This is the king Israel longed for, but they searched for him in all the wrong places and did not recognize him when he came. They supposed that sociopolitical structures of the nations might bring about the satisfaction of their souls. Israel, representing all of humanity in this sense, longed for their earthly king. They had forgotten their heavenly trajectory. Their father Abraham had sought that city "whose architect and builder is God" (Heb. 11:10), yet they had set their eyes below. They thought their longings were to be found in *their* will and *their* design. But God in his kindness was sending their King to rule all the nations in accord with *his* will and *his* design.

Jesus the God-Man was born into a land ruled by an earthly king—Herod. King Herod is a remarkable person in history. The Gospels paint Herod as a powerful yet deeply insecure and pathological egotist who is obsessed with power. And yet, in their reports Herod was a fairly normal king in human terms.

In terms of the power of a human king, Herod the Great was as successful as they come. In his own context, he had a successful reign in Judea as a vassal to the Roman Empire. His accomplishments in architecture resulted in many of his projects still standing to this day. Additionally, he defended two serious threats to his throne, before passing the seat to his sons after his death. This succession was the establishment of the "Herodian dynasty."

However, King Herod was also a pathological egotist, obsessed with power. Throughout his reign he took radical and ruthless steps to ensure that his seat on the throne was secure. Emperor Augustus is famously attributed with saying, "It is better to be Herod's pig than his son."[36] This is because in Jewish culture, one did not eat pork, but Herod slaughtered threats to his throne. When he thought someone might overthrow him, he killed them. He killed and he ordered the killing of at least one brother-in-law and one wife. His paranoid rule was characteristic of his day.[37] This is what kings had become.

Clearly, Herod was quick to remove any perceived threat to his throne. Yet the greatest threat to his kingdom came when he heard of a baby *born* King of the Jews. Herod was not born king of this people. He seized his rule by force. Herod's response is to quench this threat as he had all others:

> When King Herod heard this, he was deeply disturbed, and all Jerusalem with him. So he assembled all the chief priests and scribes of the people and asked them where the Messiah would be born.

> "In Bethlehem of Judea," they told him, "because this is what was written by the prophet:
>
> And you, Bethlehem, in the land of Judah,
> are by no means least among the rulers of Judah:
> Because out of you will come a ruler
> who will shepherd my people Israel."
>
> Then Herod secretly summoned the wise men and asked them the exact time the star appeared. He sent them to Bethlehem and said, "Go and search carefully for the child. When you find him, report back to me so that I too can go and worship him."
>
> After hearing the king, they went on their way. And there it was—the star they had seen at its rising. It led them until it came and stopped above the place where the child was. When they saw the star, they were overwhelmed with joy. Entering the house, they saw the child with Mary his mother, and falling to their knees, they worshiped him. Then they opened their treasures and presented him with gifts: gold, frankincense, and myrrh. (Matt. 2:3–11)

The wise men who were supposed to bring this child to Herod, ultimately for his demise, instead worship the child. Those who have stood face-to-face with the *ruling* king cannot help but worship the one who is *truly* King. The rule and reign of Christ is immediately obvious to those who behold it. But the sad lesson of history and human experience is that we so often yearn for God but place our hope in a human king, who cannot and will not deliver on our hopes.

Herod eventually comes to know that his secret plan has not succeeded, and so he plots something even more radical: "Then Herod, when he realized that he had been outwitted by the wise men, flew into a rage. He gave orders to massacre all the boys in and around Bethlehem who were two years old and under, in keeping with the time he had learned from the wise men" (Matt. 2:16). Herod before was so threatened by this baby that he tried to kill him. When he fails the first time, Herod shows how deeply disturbed and corrupt he truly is. He orders thousands of baby boys to be killed, all to protect his throne.

He knows that only one of these children was proclaimed the one born King of the Jews. However, Herod sees no amount of carnage as too great to protect his throne. This is all because of what Herod knows. Herod knows that he is *not* the one who has been promised. He knows he is *not* the one who will reign on David's throne. Herod's response indicates that he knows he is not this King. He knows that his throne is not going to last forever. For Herod it is not good news to hear that this baby has been born King of the Jews this day. Despite Herod's wicked plans, there is One who is sovereign over all of creation, and he ensured that his Son was safely in Egypt (Matt. 2:13–15). God's Son will reign forever, and no earthly authority will thwart God's plans. The King has come!

With the anticipation of the promised King of Israel comes the anticipation of the inauguration of the kingdom of God. Shortly after Jesus comes onto the scene, so does the inauguration of the kingdom. In Matthew 3, John the Baptist was proclaiming in the wilderness, "Repent, because the kingdom of heaven has come near!" (v. 2). In Matthew 4, Jesus begins his public ministry with the same message: "From then on Jesus began to preach, 'Repent, because the kingdom of heaven has come near'" (v. 17).

Jesus's words could have two different connotations. The first is that the kingdom coming near references its proximity in time. The kingdom is coming right now. It is right around the corner. This is probably the sense John the Baptist emphasizes, speaking of a soon-coming kingdom. Jesus, on the other hand, seems to expound on that. The kingdom coming near means it was there in front of them. The presence of Jesus himself signals that the kingdom is close. The kingdom being at hand has less to do with the immediacy of consummation of history through the inauguration of God's kingdom and more to do with the fact that Christ is King. Christ is King and the kingdom has come. He is walking amid the people and bringing with him the kingdom of God.

Back in Luke 4, when Jesus begins his earthly ministry, Jesus publicly reads of the messianic rule and declares that he is the Messiah now come:

> The scroll of the prophet Isaiah was given to him, and unrolling the scroll, he found the place where it was written:
>
> > The Spirit of the Lord is on me,
> > because he has anointed me
> > to preach good news to the poor.
> > He has sent me
> > to proclaim release to the captives

> and recovery of sight to the blind,
> to set free the oppressed,
> to proclaim the year of the Lord's favor.
>
> He then rolled up the scroll, gave it back to the attendant, and sat down. And the eyes of everyone in the synagogue were fixed on him. He began by saying to them, "Today as you listen, this Scripture has been fulfilled." (Luke 4:17–21)

Jesus begins his public ministry by reading about the reign of the Messiah and says, "I am he, and my reign is now. The Scripture has been fulfilled today, in your hearing, *by me*." Throughout Jesus's ministry his actions show him to be the promised King, whom the Jews have long awaited. One of those actions is recorded in Matthew 12. Jesus was in a field with his disciples, and they were pulling grain on the Sabbath. The Pharisees confront Jesus and claim that Jesus and his disciples are breaking the laws of the Sabbath. Jesus's response to them is absolutely remarkable. By comparing their current situation with one from the life of David, he discusses the weightier matters of the law along with his authority over the Sabbath:

> He said to them, "Haven't you read what David did when he and those who were with him were hungry: how he entered the house of God, and they ate the bread of the Presence—which is not lawful for him or for those with him to eat, but only for the priests? Or haven't you read in the law that on Sabbath days the priests in the

> temple violate the Sabbath and are innocent? I tell you that something greater than the temple is here. If you had known what this means, I desire mercy and not sacrifice, you would not have condemned the innocent. For the Son of Man is Lord of the Sabbath." (Matt. 12:3–8)

After this, they are in the synagogue where Jesus healed a man (Matt. 12:9–13) and exorcises a demon (Matt. 12:22). As these events took place, the crucial issue for Matthew compiling these events together becomes evident. The crowd is seeing Jesus and hearing his teachings and is beginning to put all the pieces together, so they ask: "Could this be the Son of David?" (Matt. 12:23). The crowds begin to recognize Jesus's teaching and preaching as coming from one who had authority, not like the scribes (Matt. 7:28–29). Additionally, they begin to see the purpose for Jesus doing miracles. They begin to watch Jesus and to listen to him, realizing that these are signs of the promised messianic rule.

It is an astounding thing when you place this event in the context of the Gospels. Jesus was often in Galilee, with his ragtag group of disciples, without any political power or sway. He was not seen as a major player. He was not yet seen as a threat to the powers that be. This does not look like a royal court. However, what Jesus says and what Jesus does lead even the crowd to speculate whether he could be David's son. Is that not amazing? Israel's longing for the Messiah was so powerful that the common people felt it in their bones.

Chapter 22

The King's Message

After many centuries of waiting and yearning from Israel, their King has arrived—the kingdom has arrived. However, the message Jesus preaches concerning the kingdom is not what we expect. In his many parables he tells us what the kingdom of God is like and what it is unlike. This is most evident in Matthew 13. Jesus references the kingdom nine times, using seven parables. Three important themes, which describe the kingdom of heaven, appear. First, the kingdom of God will not only be enormous in size, but it will fully encompass the earth: "He presented another parable to them: 'The kingdom of heaven is like a mustard seed that a man took and sowed in his field. It's the smallest of all the seeds, but when grown, it's taller than the garden plants and becomes a tree, so that the birds of the sky come and nest in its branches.' He told them another parable: 'The kingdom of heaven is like leaven that a woman took and mixed into fifty pounds of flour until all of it was leavened'" (vv. 31–33).

This is not the first time in this chapter that Jesus pairs two parables, making the same point with two different images, revealing two different emphases. Here, Jesus pairs the mustard seed and the leaven in describing the growth of the kingdom of God. Many have wondered about Jesus's use of the mustard seed over the centuries. After all, the mustard seed is not the smallest of all seeds. The mustard tree was also not the largest of all trees, growing only ten feet. The specifics of the smallest seed and the tallest tree are not most important here, but Jesus clearly had their attention, which was his purpose. The emphasis is where the mustard plant begins compared to its end. Yes, the mustard seed is of considerably small size, similar in size to other garden plants in its beginning. However, unlike normal garden plants, the mustard tree is considerably larger, and it is as if the bud has exploded. The kingdom of God is similar. It may have a meager, seemingly inconsequential beginning, but one day it will show its full size as a worldwide kingdom, ruled over by Jesus himself.

So, too, with leaven in making bread. When making bread, the leaven is added, but it is at first hardly noticed in the dough. Yet, when mixed in, it is pervasive, and its appearance once again is explosive. Leaven impacts the entire loaf and produces growth not seen at its initial introduction. But the effect of the leaven in the dough is fully evident when the bread is completely baked. The dough rises to its fullness, its completion. The kingdom of God's advance may seem initially insignificant, but it is pervasive. One day no one will be able to disregard the total all-encompassing reign of this King in his kingdom. Indeed, every knee will bow and every tongue confess that Jesus Christ is Lord (Phil. 2:10–11).

The second theme describing the kingdom of God is its exceeding value: "The kingdom of heaven is like treasure, buried in a field, that a man found and reburied. Then in his joy he goes and sells everything he has and buys that field. Again, the kingdom of heaven is like a merchant in search of fine pearls. When he found one priceless pearl, he went and sold everything he had and bought it" (Matt. 13:44–46).

Whether the treasure is found accidently or on purpose, these two parables paint a similar picture: the kingdom of God's value is unmatched. Only the kingdom of God could elicit such joy from the one who finds it. These parables do not minimize the cost. In fact, they emphasize the full-encompassing cost the kingdom requires. The kingdom is the great pearl that, once we find it, there is no need to search any longer. There is no need to hold onto anything else. The kingdom of God will cost everything, yet it will provide a contentment nothing else can give. The value of the kingdom of God is unmatched and beyond price.

The third theme present in this parable discourse describes the kingdom of God requiring judgment. This is shown in the parable of the sower (Matt. 13:1–9), the parable of the weeds (Matt. 13:24–30), and the parable of the net (Matt. 13:47–50). The kingdom of God will not be an open door for all to enter. There will be a day when the kingdom of God is fully and finally inaugurated and when all of humanity will be judged and separated into two camps. Either you will belong in the kingdom of God, or you will be cast out.

In this present age there will be an ongoing mixture of the weeds and the wheat. This mixture will continue on the earth until the end of the age. What is interesting in the parable of the sower is that three out of four soils produce no fruit. Only one, the seed in the good soil, bears lasting fruit, good fruit. Time shall reveal who bears good fruit. There will be a time of judgment when all will be made right in the world, inaugurated by our King. In the meantime, those who belong in the kingdom of God, who have given up everything this world has to offer to seize the everlasting kingdom, will experience a joy that mankind has longed for throughout history.

In his miracles—like in his parables—Jesus taught and showed what the kingdom would be like. He demonstrated a kingly dominion and authority that was the authority of the Creator. Pick any of his miracles, and it can be seen that they all point to Jesus's divine authority. Jesus demonstrated his power even over the forces of nature when he turned water into wine (John 2:1–11) and calmed the storm (Matt. 8:23–27). Jesus demonstrated his authority over any sickness or disease, healing even those that had no chance to expect healing from any other power (Luke 8:43–44). Jesus demonstrated his power over death through the raising of Lazarus (John 11:41–44) and Jairus's daughter (Luke 8:54–56). Jesus showed his greater authority as King conquering Satan's authority as ruler over the earth by casting out demons. All of Jesus's miracles were not presented to us as an example for us to follow; instead they are revelations of Christ's power. When one looks at all the miracles Jesus performed, his kingly, authoritative power is consistently on display. In that moment there is no missing the fact that all of creation belongs to him.

As John explains in his prologue, not only was Jesus the Word in the beginning, but he was with God, and was God, and all things were made through him (John 1:1–3). The Lord of creation was demonstrating his lordship through his teaching and miracles. Who can do this but the one who will sit on David's throne forever? These are unmistakable messianic signs. The Messiah has come, and he has authority over all things. Just watch him.

Chapter 23

The King on Trial

By the time we come to the trial of Jesus, his authority is unavoidable. It is interesting that when we come to the arrest and trial of Jesus, the greatest depth of understanding is demonstrated not by the Jews but by an otherwise relatively insignificant, regional governor name Pontius Pilate:

> Then Pilate went back into the headquarters, summoned Jesus, and said to him, "Are you the king of the Jews?"
>
> Jesus answered, "Are you asking this on your own, or have others told you about me?"
>
> "I'm not a Jew, am I?" Pilate replied. "Your own nation and the chief priests handed you over to me. What have you done?"
>
> "My kingdom is not of this world," said Jesus. "If my kingdom were of this world, my servants would fight, so that I wouldn't be

> handed over to the Jews. But as it is, my kingdom is not from here."
>
> "You are a king then?" Pilate asked.
>
> "You say that I'm a king," Jesus replied. "I was born for this, and I have come into the world for this: to testify to the truth. Everyone who is of the truth listens to my voice."
>
> "What is truth?" said Pilate.
>
> (John 18:33–38)

Pilate is rightly remembered most infamously as the one who does not know what truth is, but he also does not know what a king is. There is pathos in Pilate's asking Jesus in the midst of his interrogation as a prisoner, "Just between us, are you a king?" Pilot can almost see who Jesus truly is and knows his rightful place is not on a cross but perhaps on a throne. Jesus knows his throne is to come but not quite yet. He must fulfill the requirements of the law that only he can fulfill.

As Jesus is on the cross, above him was an inscription Pilate ordered that read "Jesus of Nazareth, the King of the Jews" (John 19:19). Two of the most explicit announcements of Jesus as the promised king of the line of David come at his birth and then right before his death. At one's birth and death are the places where no man is crowned, but for Jesus, whose kingdom is not temporal but eternal, his kingship is not determined by the circumstances of his coronation. He is king of yesterday, today, and forever.

When the chief priests of the Jews saw this inscription in John 19, they asked Pilate to change it. In their eyes, it would be more accurate to have the inscription, "This man said, 'I am

King of the Jews'" (John 19:21 ESV). But Pilate does not relent. Even the leaders of the Jewish people fail to see their king before them, despite his clear authority. The sign was right. Jesus is the King of the Jews—and the Lord of all creation.

One of the most astounding truths is that the king who would rule from David's throne effectively ruled first from a cross. This was not done to him. His life was not taken from him. He laid his life down for his sheep. He was a King, now crucified. Yet the most glorious reality is he is the King resurrected. As John records in his vision:

> Then I saw heaven opened, and there was a white horse. Its rider is called Faithful and True, and with justice he judges and makes war. His eyes were like a fiery flame, and many crowns were on his head. He had a name written that no one knows except himself. He wore a robe dipped in blood, and his name is called the Word of God. The armies that were in heaven followed him on white horses, wearing pure white linen. A sharp sword came from his mouth, so that he might strike the nations with it. He will rule them with an iron rod. He will also trample the winepress of the fierce anger of God, the Almighty. And he has a name written on his robe and on his thigh: KING OF KINGS AND LORD OF LORDS. (Rev. 19:11–16)

Here is a glorious picture of the coming king. This is the crucified, resurrected, and ascended king. This is the king in whom the kingdom was already present, the king who will bring the kingdom to its fullness. This is the king who will fulfill every promise of kingship found in the Scripture. This is the one who will indeed rule forever on David's throne. This is the one who will bring in the messianic reign. This is the king who will judge. Jesus is the King of kings and Lord of lords forever.

Chapter 24

The Judge

Several years ago, I wrote a book on the new atheism entitled *Atheism Remix*. About fifteen years ago, the so-called new atheism arose in a major way and attracted a lot of media attention. It was, of course, not entirely new, but it was called the new atheism because it was presented as atheism with a new face. It came with new authorities such as Richard Dawkins, Christopher Hitchens, Daniel Dennett, and Sam Harris—men known as the four horsemen of the new atheism. In the book, I outlined several important distinctions between the old atheism of people like Bertrand Russell and the new atheism of Dawkins, Dennett, Hitchens, and Harris. One of the distinctions was that they began to make pointed scientific arguments.

They claimed the authority of science, not just reason or logical positivism. It was upon science which they claimed to build their argument. Another distinction was the new atheism decided to focus more on the person of Jesus. The atheism of the first half of the twentieth century was timid when it came to Jesus. Following the lead of Protestant liberal theology, the atheists of the better part of the twentieth century wanted to make a distinction between "the nice Jesus," the moral teacher, and "the vengeful, judgmental" God of the Old Testament. This limited them to a basic argument against the Old Testament and a distance from the New Testament.

The old Protestant liberalism and the older form of atheism often tried to avoid an open critique of Jesus. The liberal theologians were glad to deny the authority of the deity they presented as vengeful and bloodthirsty in the Old Testament. They pointed to a liberal interpretation of Jesus as a moral teacher. The older atheists also accepted Jesus as a good moral teacher, but they denied his deity.

The new atheists were different in that they were willing, unlike the older atheists, to bluntly reject Jesus altogether. In a well-known debate in London, Christopher Hitchens was thrown the old argument about the mean, judgmental, bloodthirsty God of the Old Testament and the sweet Jesus of the New Testament. Christopher Hitchens took a long drag from his cigarette, looked at the audience, and said, "Only an idiot who hasn't read the New Testament could ask that question." Hitchens's honest point is exactly what we see in Revelation 19.

This is not Jesus meek and mild in the secular variant or liberal theology. Jesus is not some Freudian example of feel-good human actualization. This is Jesus the reigning King. And when Jesus the King comes back, what is he going to do?

First and foremost, he is going to do what Israel demanded of their desired king: he is going to judge. But his judgment will be absolutely righteous, and his verdict will be transformed into unconditional victory. Because of this, there are clear implications for the church today. Christ's reign is always visible in the church where the kingdom and its coming manifestation and fullness are already visible. Louis Berkoff put it this way: "The visible church is the most important, and the only divinely instituted, external organization of the kingdom."[38] He means right *now*.

At the same time, the church is also the God-given means par excellence for the extension of the kingdom of God on earth and the grand scope of biblical theology. We find the revelation of Jesus Christ as the Messiah, the royal ruler, whose kingdom is first and foremost and presently spiritual, who will in the consummation of all things be not merely spiritual but also comprehensive and cosmic.

But what does the church understand this to mean now? It means that right now we live in the already and yet awaiting the not yet. We are waiting for a coming kingdom that is already present. It was present in Christ and is now present in the church. The kingdom is visible to a fallen world in the church, in every congregation ruled by Christ and ordered by Scripture. The church is not only the sign of contradiction to the world but the true church. It is the clear and unmistakable demonstration of Christ's rule. The church is taught to pray in this light as seen in the Lord's Prayer. We are taught to pray, "Your kingdom come. Your will be done on earth as it is in heaven" (Matt. 6:10). Understanding what it means that Christ is King is to understand that we are now awaiting a messianic rule. This is how Jesus taught us to pray—*right now*!

The understanding of Christ as King relativizes not only every earthly kingdom, but it also relativizes every political ambition. No political party or political leader will bring about the Messianic Age. No one will lead whose rule is going to be perfect. None. No one who will sit on the throne forever except Jesus. Jesus is King, and he will reign victoriously forever.

We await the full consummation of the kingdom when Jesus destroys all his enemies and rules with total victory. But we do not talk about Jesus's eventual reign at the time when he is eventually King. He is King *now*. So Paul wrote, "For this reason God highly exalted him and gave him the name that is above every name, so that at the name of Jesus every knee will bow—in heaven and on earth and under the earth—and every tongue will confess that Jesus Christ is Lord, to the glory of God the Father" (Phil. 2:9–11). Even as we await his coming, he reigns now.

Chapter 25

The King's Reign Reflected

Where do we see this reign now? Every facet of our life should demonstrate a manifestation of the coming kingdom. In our daily lives and in the local church's function, we proclaim Christ's reign and the kingdom to come. As Abraham Kuyper, famed prime minister of the Netherlands and leading theological figure of his day, said: "There is not a square inch in the whole domain of our human existence over which Christ, who is sovereign over all, does not cry: 'mine!'"[39]

Our homes and families must demonstrate a manifestation of the coming kingdom. This helps explain many biblical passages we might otherwise misunderstand. Wives are to submit to their husbands as to the Lord (Eph. 5:22). Christ is the head of the church and has authority. The church submits to Christ, her head. So, too, wives are to submit to their husbands, their head. But wives do not submit unto their husbands as an end to itself but "as to the Lord." Christ reigns and has authority. The way wives relate to their husbands testifies to this or questions it. Husbands are to love their wives as Christ loved the church (Eph. 5:25). Christ gave his life for his bride, his body. Husbands are to model Christ's love in the way they nourish and cherish their bride. With his authoritative word, Christ has told husbands to love their brides sacrificially as he has his. The way husbands relate to their wives similarly testifies or questions Christ's relationship with his church. There will be a day when none marry or are given into marriage (Matt. 22:30), but our marriages in this age testify to the manifestation of the kingdom of God and Christ's reign. All this could make little sense except for this—Jesus Christ is Lord.

The way we work and relate to others should demonstrate a manifestation of the coming kingdom. We work as one who has a Master who is in heaven who rewards those who are faithful. Christ reigns. We forgive as ones who have been forgiven much by the One who reigns. To fail to do so is to misrepresent the kingdom of God. Our faithfulness is to be as a testimony to God's rule in Christ the King.

The way we spend our money and time should demonstrate a manifestation of the coming kingdom. If we are found with abundance, we are not to set our heart upon it but to be rich in good works with the abundance, for God will provide all that we need. And all that we have he has provided (1 Tim. 6:17). So too, we make the best use of our time, knowing the days are evil (Eph. 5:16). We live in light of the reign of Christ by walking in wisdom with the time we have. Someone who makes the best use of their days reflects a kingdom character that understands every moment to be from and for the Lord. Every moment!

All of our plans and dreams should demonstrate a manifestation of the coming kingdom. We cannot secure our plans, so we simply plan while understanding all is contingent on the Lord's will (James 4:15). The things we desire, the dreams we anticipate—all should be directed to the coming kingdom.

In our yearnings we demonstrate a manifestation of the kingdom of God. In the yearning that things be made right, we know the world will be made right in every respect. We know *who* will make it right, and so we yearn for his return. As C. S. Lewis said, a Christian's desires unsatisfied on earth remind us we were made for somewhere else wholly other.[40] As those made in God's image, we yearn for Christ's right rule. And our yearnings *will* be satisfied. When we rightly reflect this yearning with our present actions, we proclaim Christ's reign and the kingdom to come.

This will not lead to perfection, but our lives should encompass a sign of God's promise and blessing. All that we do should reflect a manifestation of the kingdom of God and Christ's authority. He is King over heaven and earth here, right now, and forever.

The church rightly ordered by the Word of God demonstrates the reign of Christ in the present. In the gathered church God's people hear the Shepherd's voice and obey. There the kingdom ethic is put on full display. From there the word of the King is sent to the corners of the earth to be declared. There the weary and heavy-laden have found rest in their Savior, Christ the King. There with the keys of the kingdom the King's justice is put on display.

Consider this hymn by Charles Wesley written in 1744, not in a happy time in Wesley's life. Perhaps that makes it even more meaningful when we read these words:

Rejoice, the Lord is King:
Your Lord and King adore!
Rejoice, give thanks and sing,
And triumph evermore.
Lift up your heart,
Lift up your voice!
Rejoice, again I say, rejoice!

Jesus, the Savior, reigns,
The God of truth and love;
When He has purged our stains,
He took his seat above;
Lift up your heart,
Lift up your voice!
Rejoice, again I say, rejoice!

His kingdom cannot fail,
He rules o'er earth and heav'n;
The keys of death and hell
are to our Jesus giv'n:
Lift up your heart,
Lift up your voice!
Rejoice, again I say, rejoice!

Rejoice in glorious hope!
Our Lord and judge shall come
And take His servants up
To their eternal home:
Lift up your heart,
Lift up your voice!
Rejoice, again I say, rejoice![41]

If Jesus is not King, we are doomed. If Jesus is not King, history is just one horrible thing after another. If Jesus is not King, the Messianic Age will never come. If Jesus is not King, then we are not saved. *But Jesus is King*. So we wait expectantly as his people, living as his people, until the consummation of the kingdom of God.

All praise, glory, and honor be to Christ our King.

This is Jesus. This is who he is, this is what he has done. Jesus is the Prophet, the Priest, and the King. He is all three, all the time, perfectly. He is absolutely faithful, and his reign will last forever. We live in the glory of seeing Christ in three offices—prophet, priest, and king. One day we shall see him face-to-face. Until then, by God's grace and for his glory, we press on.

About the Author

Dr. R. Albert Mohler Jr. (AlbertMohler.com) has served as President of The Southern Baptist Theological Seminary and Boyce College for more than thirty years. One of the nation's most influential theologians and public commentators, he is the host of The Briefing, a daily podcast analyzing news and events from a Christian worldview, and is editor of WORLD Opinions, where he provides regular commentary on moral, cultural, and theological issues. Dr. Mohler has authored numerous books, including *The Gathering Storm: Secularism, Culture, and the Church*, *The Apostles' Creed: Discovering Authentic Christianity in an Age of Counterfeits*, *The Conviction to Lead: 25 Principles for Leadership That Matter*, *Recapturing the Glory of Christmas*, and *Tell Me the Stories of Jesus: The Explosive Power of Jesus' Parables.* He lives in Louisville, Kentucky, with his wife, Mary, and is a proud father and grandfather.

Notes

1. Eusebius, *Eusebius' Ecclesiastical History: Complete and Unabridged*, trans. Christian Frederic Cruse (Peabody: Hendrickson, 1998), 11.

2. Eusebius, *Eusebius' Ecclesiastical History*, 13.

3. John Calvin, *Calvin: Institutes of the Christian Religion*, 2 vols., ed. John T. McNeill and trans. Ford Lewis Battles (Louisville: Westminster John Knox, 2006), vol. 1, II.xv.1.

4. Martin Luther, WA 5.163.28-9, as cited by Alister E. McGrath in *Luther's Theology of the Cross: Martin Luther's Theological Breakthrough* (New York: Basil Blackwell, 1985), 152.

5. Martin Luther, *The Bondage of the Will*, trans. J. I. Packer and O. R. Johnston (Grand Rapids: Fleming H. Revell, 1957), 67.

6. Andy Crouch, "Steve Jobs: The Secular Prophet," *The Wall Street Journal*, October 8, 2011, https://www.wsj.com/articles/SB10001424052970203476804576615403028127550.

7. Cornel West, "Prophetic Imagination: Confronting the New Jim Crow and Income Inequality in America," *Engaging Pedagogies in Catholic Higher Education*, vol. 1, no. 1 (2015), 5, https://digitalcommons.stmarys-ca.edu/cgi/viewcontent.cgi?article=1005&context=epiche.

8. "2023 God's Prophetic Words: Warnings and Preparations," *Perry Stone Ministries*, accessed February 13, 2023, https://perrystone.org/events/2023-gods-prophetic-words-warnings-and-preparations-livestream-event.

9. Ramban (Nachmanides), *Commentary on the Torah: Deuteronomy*, trans. Charles B. Chavel (New York: Shilo, 1976), 222.

10. Jonathan T. Pennington, *Jesus the Great Philosopher: Rediscovering the Wisdom Needed for the Good Life* (Grand Rapids: BrazosPress, 2020), 7.

11. Pennington, *Jesus the Great Philosopher*, 7.

12. Fred B. Craddock Jr., *As One without Authority* (St. Louis, MO: Chalice Press, 2001), 11.

13. Craddock, *As One without Authority*, 13.

14. R. C. Sproul, *John* in St. Andrew's Expositional Commentary (Lake Mary: Reformation Trust, 2009), 117–19.

15. Westminster Shorter Catechism, Question 24, see in *Reformed Confessions*, 356.

16. Herman Bavinck, *Reformed Dogmatics: Sin and Salvation in Christ*, vol. 3, ed. John Bolt and trans. John Vriend (Grand Rapids: Baker Academic, 2006), 473.

17. David R. Helm, *Expositional Preaching: How We Speak God's Word Today* (Wheaton, IL: Crossway, 2014), 44.

18. Michael A. G. Haykin, *Amidst Us Our Belovèd Stands: Recovering Sacrament in the Baptist Tradition* (Bellingham, WA: Lexham Press, 2022), 125.

19. Flannery O'Connor, "A Good Man Is Hard to Find," *The Complete Stories* (New York: Farrar, Straus and Giroux, 1971), 132.

20. Flannery O'Connor, *The Habit of Being*, ed. Sally Fitzgerald (New York: Farrar, Straus and Giroux, 1979), 465.

21. *Westminster Confession of Faith* (1647), chapter 8: "A Confession of Faith: Put Forth by the Elders and Brethren of Many Congregations of Christians (Baptized upon Profession of Their Faith) in London and the Country" (1677) 8:10 from Mike Renihan, facsimile ed. (Auburn, MA: B & R Press, 2000), 34.

22. See further Herman Bavinck, *Reformed Dogmatics,* ed. John Bolt, trans. John Vriend (Grand Rapids: Baker, 2006) 3:238–40.

23. This priestly representation can be seen among the Romans when the Roman augurs marked the ground "to watch out for signs from the gods" Mary Beard and John North, Pagan Priests: Religion and Power in the Ancient World (London: Duckworth, 1990), 8.

Additionally, this representation is seen in the history of God's people, Joel R. Beeke and Paul M. Smalley, Reformed Systematic Theology, 4 Vols. (Wheaton: Crossway, 2020), 2:992–2:993.

24. Mary Beard and John North, *Pagan Priests: Religion and Power in the Ancient World* (London: Duckworth, 1990), 13 and within the Christian tradition, Beeke and Smalley, *Reformed Systematic Theology*, 4 Vols., 2:992; John Owen, *An Exposition of the Epistle to the Hebrews* 2:14, 4:449; Augustine *Confessions* 10.43.69.

25. Though not explicitly called mediation, the augurs were given the ability to interrupt political proceedings since they had "the power to demonstrate that an assembly was not proceeding in accordance with the will of the gods." Mary Beard and John North, *Pagan Priests*, 4.

26. Augustine, "Questions on the Heptateuch" in *Writings on the Old Testament*, from *The Works of Saint Augustine: A Translation for the 21st Century* 1/14, ed. Boniface Ramsay, trans. Joseph T. Lienard and Sean Doyle (New York: New City Press of the Focolare, 2016), 2.73.

27. C. S. Lewis, *Mere Christianity* (New York: HarperCollins, 1980), III.11.

28. See "The Savoy Declaration XI" in *Reformed Confessions* 4:470; "The Second London Baptist Confession XI" in *Reformed Confessions* 4:546; Beeke and Smalley, *Reformed Systematic Theology*, 2:1037–48.

29. John Murray, *Redemption: Accomplished and Applied* (Grand Rapids: Eerdmans, 1955), 54.

30. Elvina M. Hall, "Jesus Paid It All," 1865, public domain.

31. David Toshio Tsumura, *The First Book of Samuel*, New International Commentary on the Old Testament (Grand Rapids: Eerdmans, 2007), 248.

32. Robert D. Bergen, *1, 2 Samuel*, vol. 7, New American Commentary (Nashville: B&H, 1996), 116–17.

33. John Piper, *Providence* (Wheaton: Crossway, 2021), 131.

34. Piper, *Providence*, 133.

35. Lord Acton to Archbishop Creighton in written correspondence, 1887, https://oll.libertyfund.org/title/acton-acton-creighton-correspondence.

36. From Macrobrius's second book *Saturnalia*, "Melius esse porcum Herodis quam filium," https://www.newliturgicalmovement.org/2019/01/a-medieval-fresco-of-holy-innocents.html.

37. "Mariamne," *Encyclopedia Britannica*, https://www.britannica.com/biography/Mariamne-wife-of-Herod-I.

38. Louis Berkoff, *Systematic Theology, Fourth Revised and Enlarged Edition* (Grand Rapids: Eerdmans, 1949), 409.

39. Abraham Kuyper, *Sphere Sovereignty in Abraham Kuyper: A Centennial Reader,* ed. James D. Bratt (Grand Rapids: Eerdmans, 1998), 488.

40. Lewis, *Mere Christianity*, 136–37.

41. Charles Wesley, "Rejoice, the Lord Is King!," 1744, public domain.

ALSO AVAILABLE

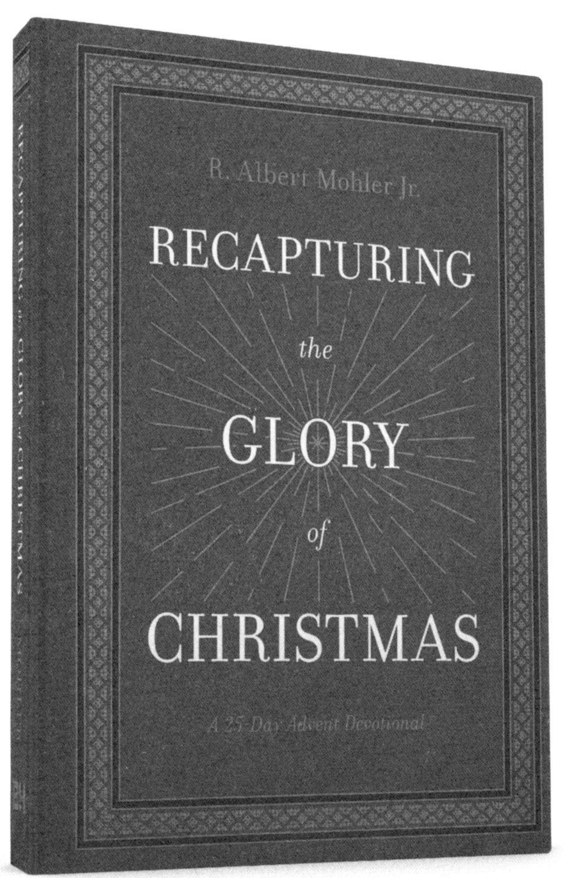

A 25-day Advent devotional from

R. Albert Mohler Jr.